Energy
Healing
^{for} Beginners

Other books by Ruth White

Working with Your Chakras
A Message of Love
Working with Guides and Angels
Chakras – A New Approach to Healing Your Life
Your Spiritual Journey
Karma and Reincarnation

Ruth White

Energy Healing
for Beginners

**A step-by-step
guide to the basics
of spiritual healing**

PIATKUS

Visit the Piatkus website!

Piatkus publishes a wide range of bestselling fiction and non-fiction, including books on health, mind, body & spirit, sex, self-help, cookery, biography and the paranormal.

If you want to:
- read descriptions of our popular titles
- buy our books over the internet
- take advantage of our special offers
- enter our monthly competition
- learn more about your favourite Piatkus authors

VISIT OUR WEBSITE AT: www.piatkus.co.uk

© 2002 Ruth White

First published in 2002 by
Judy Piatkus (Publishers) Ltd
5 Windmill Street, London W1T 2JA

The moral rights of the author have been asserted

A catalogue record for this book is available from the British Library

ISBN 0-7499-2303-2

Illustrations by Rodney Paull

Phototypeset by Action Publishing Technology, Gloucester
Printed & bound in Great Britain by Biddles Ltd
www.biddles.co.uk

Contents

Acknowledgements

I should like to acknowledge and thank all who have helped, inspired and supported me in the writing of this book:

The individuals and groups who have come to me for healing training, practice and encouragement, and those who have come to me for healing and counselling sessions. The individuals and groups who have asked all the questions that have manifested the information. My guide Gildas, for all his patient teaching and wise presence. My daughter Jane, for her unconditional love, support and encouragement. The whole encouraging team at Piatkus. My Jack Russell dog 'Jackson', now eight years old, for his sense of humour and balance and for his company whilst I type manuscripts.

Dedication

To Sue Cross – a loyal friend, inspirer and co-traveller, with love, light, fun and adventure!

Introduction

'Hello, how are you?' is probably our most common greeting to each other – and exists in most languages. 'I am well, thank you' is an equally common reply but often not an entirely honest one, since the greeting question is not usually an invitation to expand fully on our current state of health.

Yet the fact that the question is an integral part of everyday interaction indicates that how we feel in ourselves is important. Most of us know a condition of body, mind and spirit which we would describe as wellness. Equally, we are aware of various states of 'not so wellness', from slight unwellness to definite illness.

Our experience of these degrees of wellness or unwellness depends on a number of complex factors linked to body, mind, spirit and emotions. Honest answers to the greeting question 'How are you?' might include: 'A bit liverish', 'Rather down in spirits', 'Very tired', 'Quite depressed', or 'Struggling with my emotions'. Bodily symptoms may accompany emotional or mind states as well as spiritual malaise. All four ingredients intermingle, and when we first feel 'out of sorts' we may not know which of body, mind, emotions or spirit is the main contributor.

Of course, if we are really ill then bodily symptoms will probably prevail and we may need to spend some time in bed or consult a medical practitioner. When we are less than well or actively ill, we lose the ability to recharge our own fitness or energy batteries. We may need rest or relaxation of some kind to bring things back to normal or we may need specific treatment and help. Increasingly, it is accepted that treating only one part of the foursome of body, mind, spirit and emotions is rarely enough. In the same way, treating symptoms such as a headache or stomach pain on their own may not deal with the underlying cause of an illness. In such a scenario, one symptom may disappear only to give rise to another. We are complex beings, and illness or malaise arise from complex interactions within us.

Fortunately, most phases of 'not wellness' pass. Our powerful self-healing mechanisms kick in, and we feel better. We can truthfully and cheerfully answer the question 'How are you?' with 'I am very well indeed, thank you.' Sometimes, however, that self-healing mechanism fails us and treatment of our symptoms does not make us well again. When this happens, are there other energies that can give our self-healing mechanism a boost and help us to trace a true way back to health?

I believe there are. I also believe that these energies enable us to move through disease, not simply back to a place of health we have known before but onwards to a new place of health and well-being that is both different from, and better than, anything we have ever known before. These energies are healing energies and are more commonly and freely available than we may realise.

HEALING IN EARLY SOCIETIES

Healers of all kinds have always been important to the continuity of human life. Even very early tribes are known to have had specialist healers or medicine men and women. Many cultures have a special reverence for people who research the workings of the human body and who practise healing in its various forms. Early civilisations knew about herbs and other natural substances that would aid healing processes or bring relief from pain. Although much early healing was ritualistic and employed the use of 'magic', there is archaeological evidence that complex brain surgery was performed by some of our ancient ancestors. Well-preserved skulls with neatly drilled holes in them have been found in South America, suggesting that there was early knowledge (later lost) of techniques such as trepanning to relieve pressure in the brain.

Every tribe had its healer. The young were carefully assessed to see which skills came naturally to them, and the healer was as important as the hunter or the warrior. Knowledge was passed on from one generation to another in a form of apprenticeship. In Western society today, we have lost touch with the idea of looking for natural healing abilities in children – but, as we shall see in the course of this book, my work with healers has often brought people to me who have manifested a healing gift, and perhaps fulfilled a role as family healer, from quite a young age.

THE VALUE OF COMPLEMENTARY THERAPIES

Our present society relies heavily on the medical profession, as well as on scientific research, to provide healing interventions that grow ever more technical and complex. Yet in recent years there has been an upsurge in alternative or complementary therapies. Some people shun the medical approach and rely entirely on the alternatives. Others, including many doctors, think that natural therapies can be seen as complementary to the scientifically developed ones. This is a more sensible and sensitive approach. When complementary therapies are used in the healing process, it is more likely that each of those four important aspects of the being that interact to make us feel well or unwell will receive the attention it may need.

Natural therapies are complementary to one another, as well as to the conventional medical approach. Homeopathy or herbalism works alongside osteopathy or chiropractic, aromatherapy complements applied kinesiology, and natur-opathy can be supported by reflexology. Many different combinations or permutations work well together. Doctors, surgeons and complementary therapists all seek to heal. Pooled resources can have greater strength and lead to treatment of the whole being rather than the relief of symp-toms on their own.

WHAT IS 'ENERGY HEALING'?

Healers from all fields are usually very knowledgeable about the art and science of healing and make extensive studies of their favoured approaches. They advocate specific interven-tions for specific conditions. There are also healers who know intuitively that they can heal by a 'laying on of hands' or through working with the more subtle energy fields surrounding the physical body. Finding a title for this kind of healing is not easy. Some call it divine healing and draw their inspiration from a specifically religious source. Others speak of spiritual healing, which may be connected to a particular spiritual path, while others prefer to speak of energy healing. All work from a belief that there is a healing power that can be passed through one individual to another.

This belief has some foundation in the things we tend to do for each other when one of us is sick and the other well. We tend the sick. We hug or stroke a sick child or 'kiss better' an injured or aching part. We smooth pillows, put a gentle soothing hand on a painful area and prepare special foods with loving care. Such attentions are important to the healing process of the whole being. To be sick and alone is an unenviable fate.

There is a vast field between the natural skills of tending the sick (at which some people are recognisably better than others) and the wonders of modern medical science. We may not want to set up as professional healers, but many of us are interested in what we can do to help our own healing processes or those of friends and loved ones.

WHAT THIS BOOK OFFERS

This book suggests ways of extending and enhancing the natural skills, by making us more conscious of them, as well as bringing greater understanding of the many interactive factors that affect healing and disease. It is intended to appeal to a wide range of budding healers, as well as to those already in training or practice. There is something here for you if you have ever wondered whether you have healing potential but have not yet explored the field, if you are a beginner on the healing path looking for more structure, or even if you are well established in healing practice but want to revise and rethink certain aspects of the healing phenomenon.

A Personal Note

The reader may well wonder where I, Ruth the author, am coming from in writing this book. What is my personal belief system and experience of healing? In response to these natural questions and to set what I have to say in context, I should like to tell a little of my personal story.

In one sense, my life has been ordinary and mundane. I grew up with one younger brother. We had two parents who remained married and together, and lived into old age. I was educated first in a village school and then at a grammar school, took exams, went to teacher training college and became an infant school teacher. I got married at the tender age of twenty-three, had one daughter, got divorced and became a single parent when she was eight years old. I continued to teach for over twenty years, latterly as head teacher of a primary school. I never truly enjoyed teaching and was able finally to retrain as a counsellor and psychotherapist. These are skills that I practise today and which complement and inform my interest in healing.

In another sense my life has been extraordinary. For as long as I can remember, I was aware that there was another presence with me. I could sense a tall, white, shining being that seemed to me, as a child, to be an angel. For various reasons, I did not find family life easy and never felt truly bonded to my parents. Having this wondrous friend as confidant and protector helped me through some difficult years.

At first, I thought that everyone could see my angel. I saw angels or shining figures accompanying most people. I also saw colours around people, which changed when they were ill, angry or in other emotional states. I found it very strange to discover that others (particularly adults) did not see these phenomena or make any attempt to communicate with their accompanying other-worldly companions and helpers. I soon discovered that talking about what I saw made my parents very angry, so I learned to block out a lot of this vision and to keep the rest of it secret.

Pushing down these important experiences and trying to behave like the 'normal' child I was expected to be took a tremendous toll. I was not aware of being unduly stressed but, when I was fourteen, my already short-sighted eyes became more so. It was discovered that, from birth, I had actually been able to see very little with my right eye and, with the growing deterioration in my left, there were fears that I might go blind. The deterioration eventually stabilised, but it was decided that a university education would involve too much close work and I was advised to try teaching young children. (It has long puzzled me why someone threatened with deteriorating eyesight, with no desire whatsoever to teach, and with very little interest in young children, should have been considered suitable to enter a teacher training college!) At that time, in the 1950s, the main choices for educated young women were teaching, nursing or doctoring. Parents and teachers expected to have a strong influence on one's career choice; there seemed little point in arguing, and so to teacher training college I went.

At college, away from home, my inner turmoil became more obvious. I was full of fears that I hardly dared to express. My inner world was very active and the being alongside me very present. This being had always helped and supported me, but I became puzzled by my intense experience of his presence and feared I was going mad. Fortunately, I happened to be training at the only college in the country that had access to a student counsellor. My perceptive tutor suggested I might benefit from some counselling sessions. The counsellor turned out to be Mary Swainson, a Jungian psychotherapist, but also an inner brother of a spiritual and esoteric order known as the White Eagle Lodge. (Of course, I was not aware of this latter fact in my first phase of counselling and therapy with Mary.) I found that I could tell Mary about all my difficulties and, eventually, about my shining friend and my fears that I must be mad.

My childhood had been difficult and painful in many ways, and I certainly needed some basic psychotherapy. But as time went on, Mary and I talked more and more about the core experience of my life – my shining friend – and other extra-sensory perceptions that I was experiencing. She encouraged me to speak to the shining presence and to ask for a name. The replies came fluently, like a sort of dictation that I perceived clearly in my head. I wrote the words down quite quickly, as I received them.

The being told us that he wished to be called Gildas. His last incarnation had been as a monk in France in the fourteenth century and he was now able to choose whether to reincarnate or not. He was currently endeavouring to establish a link from his discarnate being to those of us in incarnation so that he could give teachings about the wider spiritual dimension of his experience and offer us a clearer or broader perspective of life on earth and the problems and dilemmas we all encounter.

My parents were members of the Congregational Church and I had always attended Sunday school. Before going to college I was a Sunday school teacher and sang in the church choir. I had never heard of reincarnation, mediumship or channelling, but I accepted that Gildas could communicate fluently with and through me. He taught about the concept of many lifetimes and I found it a natural and more comfortable model of being and evolution than any I had previously been exposed to.

Gildas readily answered the questions Mary and I put to him and, very early on, explained that he was not an angel but a guide. Guides have already incarnated and reincarnated on earth many times, and may or may not do so again. Angels have never incarnated and never will. They are manifestations of divine energies and they help and protect us in many different ways.

I believe that, before incarnating this time around, I made an agreement with Gildas to be a channel for his work. It is now over forty-three years since Mary helped me to discover and develop the means of communicating with him. Gildas is always near me, just as he was when I was a child. Now, rather than seeing him as a shining being or as a monk, I sense his presence as an energy, see his 'colours' and smell his fragrance. It takes only a few moments to make the slight shift of consciousness that enables me to receive his communications. I no longer write his words by hand, but speak them into a tape recorder or type them into my computer.

Over the years, Gildas and I have built up a working relationship. He is a friend and colleague. When we do workshops or write books, we design them together. He plays his part and I play mine. I draw on my own experience and training but it is amplified by Gildas' perspective. Subject matter is often seeded by him and he is my spiritual mentor. Much of my knowledge and practice of healing, particularly at the energetic level, has been informed and trained by him.

My first steps into healing came about when, with the support of an interested group of friends, I was developing my ability to channel Gildas. When one of the group felt unwell, Gildas suddenly suggested that she might like to receive some healing energy. I stood in Gildas' energy field, which became very strong and even more expanded than in my usual channelling contact with him, whilst the patient sat on a chair in front of me. I put my hands gently on her shoulders and was aware of being a vehicle for a special energy: I could 'see' colours flowing from my hands and around the patient. Gildas explained that I was channelling and earthing the healing energy he wanted to contribute. Afterwards, the patient felt much better, I was energised, not drained, and the whole group expressed a sense of having been part of something rather special.

From this point, Gildas gave more teaching about healing, both theoretical and practical (see my book *The Healing Spectrum*). As my work developed, I began to travel abroad to give workshops and formed several healing groups in other countries (Germany, Holland, France, Hungary and Belgium). For some years I was co-founder and teacher of the International School of Healing (unfortunately now closed) which held courses in the South of France.

When channelling healing, I am always aware that Gildas is near and often an active participant in the healing process. However, my belief and further experience is that we are both participant in channelling a more generalised healing energy, freely available in the universe.

Channelling healing and channelling a guide are not the same thing: it is not necessary to have a guide in order to be a healer or to be a healer in order to have a guide. I teach channelling as well as healing, but prefer to treat each as separate, but sometimes related, skills. Gildas is a teacher and I have based much of my healing practice on his advice and information.

What I have to say in this book comes from more than forty years of training and experience, and combines a rich input from my psychological and psychotherapeutic training and practice, teaching from Gildas, and my experience as a channel, writer, spiritual teacher, healer, and trainer of healers and channellers.

Chapter 1

I Think I Can Heal

*Stella's story – What is healing? – Healing as a natural gift –
Can anyone heal? – Can I train myself? And how do I begin? –
Making a start – Exercises – Establishing a healing flow*

STELLA'S STORY

This story is similar to many that I have heard. Stella was the oldest of four children and already had two young brothers and a sister by the time she was six years old. After the youngest baby was born, Stella's mother often felt tired, or had backache or a headache. When her mother had to sit or lie down for a while, Stella would put a hand on her head, or gently stroke her back. It seemed quite natural to her to do this and very soon her mother recognised that Stella had a healing touch. She told Stella that her hands had eased the pain and afterwards she felt a 'new woman': calmed, re-energised and ready to do the many jobs her family needed, as well as to play with her children and enjoy motherhood.

Soon it was well known in the wider family that Stella had a gift for easing aches and pains and soothing a fevered brow. Sensibly, her mother protected Stella from being asked to help too often or being regarded as different, special or strange. Over the years, as Stella became more deeply involved in her schooling, exams and getting a place at university, her gift was called upon less and less. There were occasional suggestions that she might want to study nursing or medicine, but no one tried to press her into a mould. Her own preference was for anthropology. While going to university, getting involved in reading for her degree and then travelling for research purposes, Stella herself almost forgot, or perhaps discounted, her earlier healing gift.

It was only when Stella married and put her academic career on hold in order to be a full-time mother that she chanced to pick up a book on healing. It made her think again about her earlier experiences. She had been shown at an early age that she had an aptitude for healing. Now she wondered whether the time had come to understand more about it.

Like many people, Stella did not want to become a professional healer, but she did want to explore her healing potential. She wanted to know more about the nature of healing and find out how she could use a natural gift more efficiently, knowledgeably and responsibly, in order to help her husband, her children and others close to her, as well as herself.

Stella had a number of questions; the first of these, at one level the most direct, simple and obvious, was:

WHAT IS HEALING?

This is the first question that anyone wanting to know more about healing is likely to ask. At one level, it is the most direct, simple and obvious question, but anyone attempting to answer it must start by exploring what is in the mind of the questioner, for healing is not only an energy but also a process or journey. The journey enables movement from dis-ease to health. Channelling or harnessing the energy of healing can lead to enablement of that journey.

If the questioner has already shown a natural healing ability, they may ask, 'When I put my hands on someone what happens that is in some way different from someone else doing the same?' They are asking about healing as an energy or power. Questions about healing as a journey may come later.

Our bodies are, essentially, self-healing organisms or mechanisms. We have an immune system that helps us to stay healthy and resist infection. When we get minor illnesses, like colds, digestive upsets or a passing headache, we get better by a natural process. This process may be helped if we can take some rest when we feel 'off colour' so that our bodies can concentrate on coming into balance again, but for minor ailments we usually do not need to take medication or see a doctor. 'I'm a bit out of sorts today – but I will be better tomorrow' is a statement that reflects our faith in the ability of our bodies to recover.

When we get more seriously ill, something seems to happen to our self-healing process. We don't 'bounce back' and we reach a stage where we know that help is required to 'make us better'. We usually go to a doctor for such help and are given advice, perhaps some medication and permission to take things more easily for a while.

We might also look for help from the field of complementary medicine, where there are many different approaches to be considered. They are often based on ancient wisdom and complement or offer alternatives to medication and interventions based on chemical formulae or surgery. Some methods, such as acupuncture, use little or no medication, while others recommend fragrances, herbs, minerals, vitamins or food supplements. Homeopathy uses both natural and apparently toxic or disease-related substances in such minimal dilution that the contents of a finished homeopathic preparation are difficult to ascertain by scientific analysis. At base, all forms of healing intervention have one thing in common – to kickstart the self-healing process.

HEALING AS A NATURAL GIFT

The sort of healing that Stella did naturally as a child has the same aim as any other kind of healing intervention: to help a body that is ill, in pain or out of sorts, to restore itself to normality. 'Hands-on' healers may sense some energy or vitality flowing through them and being transmitted to, and accepted by, the one requiring healing. Whether or not this energy is actually felt and identified by either party, this is what appears to happen.

What is the origin of this energy? Does it come from the healer in person? Or from some other source? The belief that healing comes from some other source results in it often being associated with faith, church, the divine or religion. It is frequently called 'faith healing', 'divine healing' or 'spiritual healing'. Such associations enhance its benefits for some, but can form a barrier for others who do not consider themselves to be religious or spiritual.

We do not have to be religious or spiritual to recognise that there are energies and forces within the universe that affect us both positively and negatively. If we think of our bodies as organisms that are, on the whole, self-healing, then it is not too big a philosophical step to imagine that there are forces outside as well as inside ourselves that nurture health and healing.

There are natural, universal energies that are, indeed, divine and spiritual in the widest sense, but which do not have to be directly linked to a specifically religious faith or belief. What makes a tree grow, a plant flower, a baby gestate and come to birth? There is something more than the seed in the earth or the meeting of ovum and sperm that perpetuates the process. So also with healing and recovery from disease, there is something 'other' involved in the process. If that 'other' can be harnessed, then we can help our own and our fellow human beings' healing process.

There are healers, sometimes called 'magnetic healers', who consciously build up their own vitality and then allow the one being healed to draw on what has been built up. For them, the giving of healing can be a draining, devitalising experience and they need time to recharge before healing again or even before going about the business of normal, everyday life.

For other healers, healing does not come from their own vitality. It has to be channelled in some way. These healers are able to let that something 'other' that exists within the universe flow through them and into another. They feel vitalised, not drained, when they have given healing.

A rather mundane analogy for the process of healing via a healer is that of a flat car battery. It can be recharged by attaching jump leads from a car with a healthy battery and allowing energy to flow through the leads into the flat battery. A magnetic healer might see themselves as the healthy battery, connected to the depleted one and giving it energy. The other vision is to see the healthy battery as the universal source and the healer as the jump leads, providing a connection and a channel from that source to the flat battery, and so enabling it to vitalise itself.

This then, is healing energy most simply defined: the sensing of an available force that can be channelled through our hands to another human being (or maybe an animal) whose self-healing mechanism is temporarily disabled.

Healers can, and do, learn a variety of energetic techniques and interventions, but many eventually return to the most simple – being a channel for healing energy. But, although this is where many begin and the point to which many return, the exploration of healing at and from subtle levels is wide and rich.

CAN ANYONE HEAL?

Through helping and training healers, I have found that, almost without exception, anyone who really wants to heal can do so. If the impulse and the desire are sufficiently strong to make you look seriously at even the simplest ways of developing your healing skills, something in you is urging you to recognise, use and develop a natural gift.

In one sense it is true that healers are born rather than made: although training can help in directing, applying and perfecting a natural gift, it cannot implant a basic flair or aptitude that is not already in existence. It is the same in most areas of life. I have been taught to play the piano and can do so well enough to amuse myself, but I shall never be a pianist because the natural bent is not there. Some people take up a brush and paint beautifully with little tuition. When they are taught, their techniques, perspective and artistic approach may blossom more consciously, but the basic gift is inborn. As in every field of giftedness, there will always be those healers who have an extra flair, but training will enhance natural skills, broaden knowledge and increase understanding of the healing process.

Some people become aware that they have a gift at an early age, but those who have not had such premanifestation but who nevertheless get a definite urge to look at what being a healer means should regard this urge as a prompting to explore something that is waiting to be acknowledged and brought to fruition.

CAN I TRAIN MYSELF? AND HOW DO I BEGIN?

It is possible to self-train, but the second part of this question indicates the need for some guidelines, some scheme to which to refer and, perhaps, a mentor to help you along the way. This book encourages you to use and develop basic healing skills, but if you want to train more extensively as a healer, then you need to find a course, a mentor or an apprenticeship (see Useful Addresses, page 196).

Initially, you may want to explore healing in a natural, simple way, mainly with family and friends. You may want to find out more about what is happening, both to you and your patient, when you are healing, and to learn what to do with your hands and thoughts.

People describe varied experiences when the healing is flowing through them. Some experience a tingling or a flow in their hands; others may be aware of an infusion of energy coming from above them and down their spine, of a feeling of quietness coming upon them and surrounding them. Sometimes people feel none of these things and may simply have very mundane thoughts or conversations with whoever they are healing.

MAKING A START

It is important to do some simple energetic exercises to strengthen your awareness of energy flows. You also need a basic understanding of the subtle energy system. Many healers (given permission) touch their patients. Others touch only very lightly or work entirely in the auric energy field. Whichever method or combination you eventually choose, it is essential to broaden your experience and understanding of subtle energetic connections.

Training and practice give the healer the tools to interpret energy sensations received in the hands or the personal auric field as a session is taking place. The following exercises build from exploration, through preparation and rounding off, to a simple, structured healing intervention. They are about getting used to energy flowing through you – like a 'warm up'. (It is a good idea to read to the end of the chapter before starting to do the exercises.)

Exercise
Sensing the Energy Field, or Aura

This exercise is intended as an introduction to the complex subject of the subtle energy system, which is discussed further in the next chapter. Generally, the auric or energy field occupies a space of 10–15 centimetres (4–6 inches) around and beyond the physical body. (It also inter-penetrates with the physical body.)

   When you work with a partner in the way described in the second exercise below, you may find that you can eventually pick up each other's energy field at a much greater distance. When we are relaxed or in our own surroundings we fill more energetic space.

Working Alone

Rub the palms of your hands together for a few moments and then hold them about 1 metre (3 feet) apart. Gradually bring the palms of your hands closer and closer together until you feel a tingling sensation or slight resistance. This tingling or resistance indicates one edge of your energy field meeting the other, or the energetic poles (+ and –) interacting.

Working with a Partner

When you feel ready to do so and there is someone else to work with, each rub your own hands together (as above). Facing each other so that the right hand approaches the left and vice versa, bring your hands in from a distance to meet those of your partner. Again, as you encounter the edge of another energy field, you will be aware of a tingling or slight electrical resistance.

'GROUNDING' AND 'ENERGETIC SEPARATION'

You need to become aware of two basic principles of healing: 'grounding' and 'energetic separation'. These are important rules for would-be healers and must be practised faithfully. Although the energetic factors involved in healing are subtle, they are also strong and require respect. It is all too easy for a healer and therefore the patient or receiver of the healing to become ungrounded, light-headed and in an altered state of consciousness. In order for the transition from the healing experience back to the everyday world to be smooth and natural, grounding and energetic separation are essential.

Grounding or running energy (see exercise, page 20) is a preparation for healing. It strengthens your connection to earth, establishes a smooth flow within a central energy column running from head to feet and interpenetrating with the physical body, increases your sense of gravity and gives you balance. During the process of instigating this, the healer becomes centred, calm and receptive, a confident vehicle, enabler and transformer for the flow of universal healing energy. A healer prepared in this way will already have an energetic effect on the client/receiver, who will also become calm, centred and receptive.

In technical terms, this condition of receptivity and calmness occurs when our brains produce more alpha rhythms (as distinct from beta, delta or theta rhythms). Maxwell Cade, a researcher into altered states of consciousness, bio-feedback and human potential who, together with co-researcher Nina Coxhead, wrote the book *The Awakened Mind* (see Further Reading, page 195), designed a 'mind mirror'. When a healer and patient were connected to this mirror it was possible to demonstrate how the brain patterns changed as the healer attuned, and how the patterns from the patient were then affected by this change.

Energetic separation (see exercise, page 23) is a rounding

off after healing. It is essential to round off or make an energetic separation if you are not to be affected, even slightly, by
the symptoms of your patients. Healers in the very early
stages of practice, perhaps where no guidance has yet been
received, often report a headache, or aching shoulder or
knee, after giving healing. The presenting symptoms from
the patient are mildly replicated in the healer for some hours
afterwards. (Sometimes these replica symptoms are
mirrored, the healer, having healed a right leg, getting
aching in their own left leg, for example.) Healers have to
learn not to be 'blotting paper', and a properly visualised
energetic separation is the principal way in which to avoid
this.

Exercise
Grounding and Running Energy

Parallel to our physical spine, there is a central column of
subtle energy. To maintain balance, groundedness and good
energetic health, energy should run freely through this
column in two directions. (There is further reference to this
central energy column in the sections on energy centres, or
chakras, in Chapters 2 and 5, and in the illustration on page
21.) Imagining, breathing and visualising this energy flow
helps it to be vital. Before giving a healing of any kind, attention to this energy flow helps grounding.

This exercise is also useful as a general relaxation technique or preparation for meditation. It is essential as a
preparation for working with your chakras, which many
healers like to do in order to strengthen their energy bodies
(see Chapters 2 and 5).

You would usually do the exercise twice: once in private,
as part of the preparation for giving a healing, and again,
more briefly, as a renewal, when you are standing close to
your patient attuning for the healing. Eventually, as you

gain confidence in being with patients, you might want to teach them this exercise and do it with them.

Once with your patient, you would normally stand for this exercise, but in private you can stand or sit. Have your spine straight and your body balanced. Do not cross your legs if you are sitting in a chair, or your ankles if you are sitting on the floor (lotus or 'cross-legged' posture excepted).

Relaxation position when patient is not present.

Non-visual Method

- Begin by being aware of the rhythm of your breathing and letting it slow down a little.
- Now draw the breath in as though it comes from just above the crown of your head: draw it down through the centre of your body, just in front of your spine; change to the out-breath at a point that feels natural for you, which will probably be around the solar plexus area but may be higher or lower, and breathe out as though right

down and through your legs and into the earth. (If you are in a cross-legged or lotus position, the breath will not go down through your legs but straight out through your perineum area and into the earth, but these postures automatically balance energies in the body.) Breathe in this way about five times (i.e. five breath sequences: in/out = one sequence).

- Now, on the alternate breath sequence begin to breathe up from the earth, through the centre of your body, letting the out-breath go up through the crown of your head. Continue to breathe in this way, without straining or forcing, for about five minutes. Always end on the downward breath sequence, repeating it in this direction more than once if you wish, as you finish.
- Feel the balance of your body and then proceed to prepare for and greet your patient, or to the giving of the healing.

Visual Method

If you like visualisation and want to vary the exercise, particularly when using it as a general preparation for healing, here is a visual version. If the outdoor conditions are favourable and there is a suitable tree that you know, it is good to do this exercise in a standing position, with your back against it and your bare feet on the earth. At other times follow the posture instructions given in the above exercise.

- Begin by being aware of your breathing rhythm and let it steady and perhaps slow down a little.
- Visualise yourself as a tree. Your branches stretch out above, your roots stretch deeply into the earth, your trunk is straight and strong. You are nurtured by the four elements: sun (fire) warms you and air refreshes you. Your roots are in the earth. They seek the underground streams and sources of living water.

- Breathe in through your branches, from the elements of air and sun, take the breath right down through your trunk and breathe out strongly into your roots, into the earth and the streams of living water.
- Breathe in now from the earth and the living water, bring the breath up through your roots, through your trunk, into your branches and breathe out into the elements of air and sun.
- Repeat these two breath sequences for five to ten minutes. Then gradually let the visualisation fade. Feel your feet firmly on the ground, your own space all around you and proceed with a sense of centredness to your normal activities.

Exercise
Energetic Separation

This exercise is vital both to maintaining your own energetic health and vitality as a healer and to helping the patient use the received healing energy fully. During a healing, your energies mingle with those of your patient and, at the end, each of you needs to be firmly in your own energetic space once more. It should also be used after exploration exercises with a friend or partner (see pages 18 and 20).

When healing, you will gradually learn to recognise when the healing flow is diminishing but, in any case, simple healing sessions should not last more than twenty minutes. So either as you sense the diminishing flow, or as the specified time comes to an end, do the following:

Non-visual Method

If you find visualisation difficult, step back from your patient, give mental thanks for the privilege of the healing flow and, as above, drop your shoulders and let your arms hang loosely and relaxed by your sides with your palms slightly curled and facing inwards. Say, mentally, 'I enclose you in an egg of bright white light and myself in a separate egg of bright white light, with blessings on this energetic separation.' The power of the words will achieve separation as effectively as when visualisation is used.

Visual Method

• Step back from your patient, give mental thanks for the privilege of the healing flow, drop your shoulders and let your arms hang relaxed and loose by your sides, with the palms of your hands slightly curled and facing inwards.

*Visualisation of healer and patient
surrounded by egg shape of light.*

- Breathe in deeply from the point above your head and then out and deeply into the earth two or three times (always starting from the point above your head and not drawing up from the earth). As you do so, visualise your patient enclosed in an egg of bright white light (see illustration, opposite). Visualise a separate egg of white light surrounding you and be aware of the space between your egg of light and your patient's egg of light.

Remember that these eggs of light around you ensure that you are each within your own energetic space once more. This procedure also helps both of you make a smooth transition to the demands of normal life from any altered state of consciousness that may have taken place during the healing. The egg of light around the patient also ensures that the healing energy is contained, rather than dissipated, and will continue to be absorbed for as long as possible.

Exercise
Establishing a Healing Flow

For this sequence, I suggest that you find a co-operative friend with whom to experience and practise the previous three exercises. In essence, if the healer is well prepared and attuned, the healing starts and effects are felt from the moment that the attunement and grounding are complete. Although there are many other interventions to consider and learn, a successfully attuned healer is already generating a healing interaction. The exercises on pages 18–25 can be put together to form the basis of a simple healing sequence.

Begin by having your patient sitting comfortably on an upright chair, legs uncrossed, feet firmly on the ground. (If the chair is a little high for the patient, have a cushion or a small stool on which they can put their feet comfortably. For reasons of grounding, it is important that the whole of the foot is flat and in contact with a cushion or the floor.) Throughout this sequence, you do not touch the patient; this is a way of establishing the healing flow between two people.

Step 1

Standing behind your patient, begin by rubbing the palms of your hands together and sensing the meeting point between each side of your own energy field (see page 18).

Step 2

Remain standing behind your patient, and do the energy grounding and running exercise (see page 20).

Continue to stand behind your patient, sensing the calmness and flow that has come from the grounding and energy running, and encapsulating yourself and your patient in this flow.

Step 3

Make the energetic separation (see page 23).

This is the simplest sequence to establish a conscious healing energy flow between two people. The healer's preparation sets an energy flow in action and, when healer and patient are within that energy flow, the process of giving healing has already begun. The healer need do nothing more except the energetic separation for rounding off. The next and subsequent chapters explore ways to build on this basic structure.

Chapter 2

Getting Started

The subtle energy field, or aura – Working in the energy system –
The chakras – Practical considerations – Carrying out a
healing session – Exercises

The previous chapter described how to establish a healing
flow between two people. This chapter builds from this, and
introduces touching the patient. It is important, even in
informal healing, to have a sense of how you want to use
the healing energies to help your patient and to develop a
healing sequence that has a rhythm and pattern to it.

A subtle or basic step forward from the sequence described
on page 25 is to step nearer to your patient at the beginning
of the session and hold your hands on or near the shoulders
or head. This makes a stronger contact between healer and
patient and is already more personal and specific than
merely establishing a healing ambience.

Obviously if your patient has an ache or discomfort somewhere in the body it will usually help if the healer's hands
are placed on or above that painful part. Most patients want
healing for a specific complaint or symptom, and attending
to that is important within the healing sequence. Yet there

are other considerations that the healer using or channelling healing energy needs to be aware of, address and incorporate into even the most simple of healing interventions.

THE SUBTLE ENERGY FIELD, OR AURA

There is an energy field, or aura, around each one of us. The space we occupy does not end with the skin that surrounds our physical bodies. Our perception of what is going on around us is relayed to us by more than our senses of sight, hearing, smell, touch and taste. If we are led into a silent, unknown room with our eyes closed, we will sense whether the room is bare or furnished and usually get a good impression of its size. We sense when someone is standing behind us, not only because we hear or smell a presence but also because we are aware of a subtle response when others have stepped into our aura. This response may come as a slight shiver or tingle, or as a knowledge that a boundary around us has been crossed.

This aura is flexible. We do not physically have to take up all our energetic space – but most people feel happier and healthier in normal day-to-day interaction if there is space around them and if they know that other people are respecting that space. When we are in a crowd, we need energetic space as well as physical breathing space. Most of us find crowds exhausting and demanding because when we are packed closely together our auras are forced to mingle; under such circumstances, it is more difficult for us to 'contain' ourselves than when we are alone.

In intimate and special relationships we share our energetic space with another – willingly, joyfully or passionately – and benefit from that sharing and interaction. Crowds give us sensate overload that registers in our aura and we need time to recoup. Being in crowds or strange surroundings causes our auras automatically to draw more closely around

The aura.

us. People who are particularly sensitive in crowds and strange places may need to practise consciously gathering in their aura, so as to be more contained and less vulnerable to picking up too many impressions and energies from others at any one time.

The aura around us carries a slight electrical charge. Auras can be sensed and/or seen. People who see auras either sense a whitish light around others or see colours that change or vary with people's mood and state of health.

It may take a little training to learn to perceive auric colours but many people can see the light of the auric field, given the right conditions. Ask a friend to stand against a well-lit, lightly coloured wall; after a few moments of looking at and just beyond the line of body or clothes, your eyes may become slightly blurry with the effort of looking and you will see a subtle light around and defining the body shape. This is the aura. The development of an in-depth healing session is related to understanding the aura and its contribution to states of health and disease.

WORKING IN THE ENERGY SYSTEM

When healers work in the energy system, they work beyond the symptoms as well as with them and are able to discern the deeper causes of disease and pain. When the energy system is harmonious, the self-healing mechanisms within each one of us work more forcefully and enable our health-fulness. Allopathic medicine and surgical intervention has often been criticised for being 'symptom orientated'. It is natural to ask or expect any healer, allopathic or comple-mentary practitioner to 'take away the pain and discomfort'. Yet there are often complex causes underlying the symp-toms, the pain and the disease itself.

On my wall, I have a chart listing the Bach Flower Remedies. It gives the following advice: 'Treat the person, not the disease, the cause, not the effect.' Homeopathy is one of the complementary therapies that seeks to find 'constitutional remedies', and the same remedy is not necessarily given for similar symptoms. Chapter 4 presents a philosophy of disease and suggests ways of understanding the malaises which beset us more deeply. For now, it is enough to remember that as, basically, we are self-healing mechanisms, the root of all our troubles, whether of body, soul, spirit, emotions or mind, is that this self-healing faculty is under-functioning. If it is given an energetic boost or triggered into activity, then natural healing could potentially set in once more and our recovery should be under way. In holistic healing, the self-healing mechanism includes, but is more than, the physical immune system.

Thus, at the most basic level, a healer working with subtle energies is aiming to re-establish the vitality of the inner tendency to self-heal so that the patient journeys naturally from disease (or dis-ease) to health. A manifestation of this may be that the pains or symptoms are eased. But healing should not be regarded as something that is necessarily immediate, magical or miraculous. The movement from disease to health is a journey. The professional healer trains to accompany this journey with support, understanding and, perhaps, more complex healing intervention. The non-professional healer, working with family and friends for the most part, seeks to invoke healing energies and forces so that the journey to health can be enabled. (All healers should aim to work co-operatively with whatever other treatment may be needed and should never seek to replace the advice and diagnosis of trusted medical practitioners.)

With this very basic intention of energising the self-healing mechanism in mind, and with growing awareness of the nature of the subtle energy field, the healing session can be built into something that has shape, grace, beauty and effectiveness.

THE CHAKRAS

Much of the colour and energy of the auric field is supplied by subtle energy centres known as chakras. (The word 'chakrum' is Sanskrit and means 'wheel'. Properly speaking, chakrum is the singular form and chakra the plural, but in the West it is more usual to speak of one chakra and many chakras.) These are the points where universal energy enters and interpenetrates with our personal energy systems. For anyone able to see or sense chakras, they are wheels of light and colour that both affect and are affected by the physical body. Most chakras carry links to specific parts of the glandular system and might therefore be described as subtle glands.

Nadis and Meridians

Another Sanskrit word, 'nadis', refers to the lines of force forming intangible layers and networks of energy that are the main substance of the subtle layers or bodies surrounding each one of us. The places where these lines or nadis are produced and at which they intersect are the chakras.

The major chakras occur where many of these lines are produced and cross each other. Minor chakras are formed where the crossing and production points are less busy. Nadis are tiny, sensitive energy lines and there are many of them in the energy field. Meridians are wider and more powerful energy pathways, but also originate from, and have crossing points within, the major chakras. A simple analogy is to consider the major chakras as major roundabouts in a traffic system, with the nadis as minor roads and the meridians as major roads.

The Locations of the Chakras

There are 'echoes' of all the chakras in the palms of the hands. Flexing the hands awakens, or opens, these chakras, sets their energy buzzing and enables you to experience your own subtle energy activity (see Sensing the Energy Field, page 18). Healers use their hands to balance chakra and auric energies in order to activate the patient's self-healing mechanisms.

There is more reference to the subtle energy system (often referred to as subtle anatomy) in Chapter 6, but in order to get started the non-professional healer needs only to know where the chakras are located. The illustration on the next page shows eight chakra points and their positions in relationship to the physical body. In descending order, the chakras are named as: crown, brow, alter major, throat, heart, solar plexus, sacral and root. The names do not need to be memorised. Working without too much theoretical knowledge gives you the opportunity to develop your own impressions and instincts in relationship to each chakra and aspect of the energy field.

The chakras are major places where blocks form in our energy systems. If we learn to sense where they are and what they feel like, we can discern where or how they are out of balance and focus healing into these specific points.

Chakra Petals and Stems

In esoteric teachings there is sometimes a lack of agreement as to whether chakras are situated in the front or the back of the body and its auric field. There are systems placing some at the front and some at the back. The illustration on page 34 depicts the way in which chakras exist both in the energy field and in interpenetration with the physical body.

The exercise on page 20 gave instructions for grounding and running energy. Visualising the up and down breath awakens and energises a central subtle column of energy interpenetrating with the physical body and running from the crown of the head to the perineum (the area midway between the anus and the genitals).

Each chakra has something of the appearance of a flower, having petals and a stem. The stems of the crown and root chakras are open and are contained within the central column. The other chakras have petals opening into the auric field at the front and stems projecting into the auric field at the back.

The stems normally stay closed but the petals are flexible, opening and closing, vibrating and turning, according to the different life situations encountered. A healthy chakra is a flexible chakra. Where there is dis-ease, the chakra structures may become inflexible or actually blocked. Directing healing energy into the chakra areas can therefore aid physical, mental and emotional health.

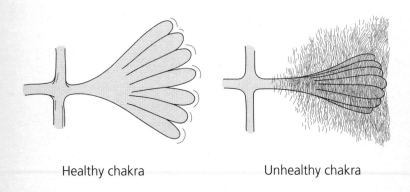

Healthy chakra   Unhealthy chakra

A healthy chakra has flexible petals that open and close.
A diseased chakra can become inflexible and
clogged, with darkened energy.

Polarities for Healing

The petals of each chakra are electrically the positive pole (+) and the stems the negative (–). Only the alter major chakra has a reversed polarity. In most people, whether left or right handed, the right hand will hold the positive electrical charge (+) and the left hand the negative (–). In order to balance the energy of the chakras, the healer usually places the right hand over the chakra petals and the left over the stems.

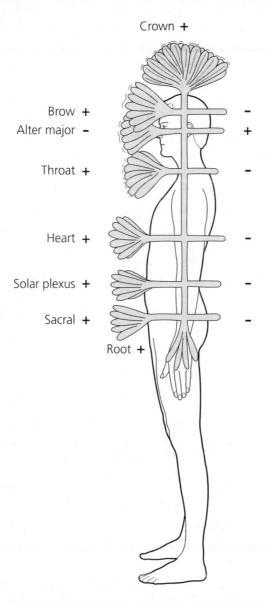

Crown **+**

Brow **+**
Alter major **–**

Throat **+**

Heart **+**

Solar plexus **+**

Sacral **+**

Root **+**

–

+

–

–

–

–

The seven best-known chakras, plus the alter major.
Energy flows both from positive (+) to negative (–)
polarities and up and down the central column.
Note the reversed polarity of the alter major chakra.

PRACTICAL CONSIDERATIONS

With some basic knowledge of the energy field, the non-professional healer is ready to make some practical preparations for a healing session. The professional healer often has a particular room or a space in which healing is frequently given. There will probably be a healing couch and there will certainly be a chair on which a patient can sit, comfortably supported, to receive healing.

The non-professional healer usually has to improvise. It is unlikely that there will be a couch (of the kind often used for massage) available and the best chair, in a home setting, will probably be a wooden dining chair or a kitchen stool. A dining chair gives back support and may be made more comfortable using cushions. A stool is, in some ways, easier for the healer, who then has free access to all the energy centres, but it may not be sufficiently comfortable or supportive for the patient. Whatever is chosen, it is important for the patient to feel that they can be comfortable in that position for twenty minutes to half an hour. For instructions on healing a patient who is lying down, see page 42.

To this end, as well as for reasons of grounding, a sitting patient's feet should be in close contact with the ground. Rather than have the patient's feet dangling or only the tips of their toes able to reach the ground, put a footstool or cushion under their feet and make sure that the whole foot is lying flat with both feet comfortably apart, and neither ankles nor knees crossed. (If the ankles and knees are crossed, the energy lines in the lower part of the body will also cross, thus affecting polarities.)

Since energy interpenetrates with matter, there is no need for the patient or healer to remove their shoes, but it may be more comfortable for both to do so. In this event, attention should be given to keeping the feet warm and it is a good idea to have warm socks available. A patient may lose body heat during a healing session, and a blanket or wrap should also be kept to hand.

As a non-professional healer, you might need to treat a patient who is lying on a settee, or ill enough to be in bed. Once some basic techniques have been learned they can be adapted to the circumstances. Beyond the simplest energetic healing exercises there are others, only slightly more complex, that are particularly suited to patients who are lying down. One is given in this chapter, on page 42; see also Drawing Out Negative Energy, page 138.

CARRYING OUT A HEALING SESSION

For your first attempts at giving a structured healing, it is best to have your patient sitting as comfortably as possible on an upright chair or stool (see page 36). If your patient has asked for healing of specific aches, pains or particular areas of the body, check that they are happy for you to touch those areas of the body lightly when the time comes. Explain that you will first be doing some healing in their energy system and that you will attend to specific aches and pains towards the end of the healing session.

Genital areas are avoided when touching a patient, as also, for a woman, are the breasts. Use your intuition about which areas to touch, in addition to any that have been specified as giving pain or trouble. You will gradually develop an intuition or sensitivity about how long to keep your hands in any one place, but usually this will not be for longer than five minutes. Applying pressure should be avoided and all movements should be very gentle. I have heard numerous complaints from people coming away from healings where they felt the healer was leaning on them rather heavily – so make sure you don't use your patient as a prop or support and that you are well balanced or have a suitable stool on which to sit if the healing is a longer one or you easily tire when standing.

Once you are carrying out fuller healing sessions you will need to leave time for talking to your patient both before and after a session. Beforehand, you would discuss the reasons why healing is required, explaining what you are going to do, ask permission if you intend to touch the physical body as well as working in the energy field, explain that although the healing is usually conducted in silence your patient should tell you immediately of anything that happens that is not comfortable for them, and that although, in general, the patient should be still, it is also all right to move or cry, or have an energy release.

Usually patients feel a great sense of calm when they are being healed and relax into a somewhat sleepy state. It is not unusual though for the healing to touch emotional levels held in the body and then the patient may shed tears, moan, move, cry out, make other sounds or shudder. The healer may need to step back for a moment to allow this to happen or simply stay in gentle touch contact for a few moments longer than usual. Remember that the patient may need a tissue for the tears, or occasionally for the healing to be interrupted in order to have a glass of water and/or talk a little before continuing.

After the healing, your patient may need tea or water and time to return from the healing experience before going about normal life once more. This is the time when you can ask what your patient experienced and also report anything you felt or sensed during the healing session.

Your first practise healing sessions should preferably last not longer than twenty minutes, so bear this in mind as you time your movements from one chakra to the next. It means that no more than about two minutes should be spent in any one area of the body. You may sense an end to the flow into the chakra you are working on, which might come as a change in temperature or energy flow, an inner knowing, or an earthy awareness that enough time has passed.

Exercise
Healing Sequence 1, with Patient Sitting

If possible, practise the following healing sequence with a friend or partner before using it with someone less well known to you.

- Stand a little behind your patient, rub your hands together to activate your hand chakras and do the grounding exercise (see page 20). As well as being necessary to the healer's energetic alignment, this grounding is a preparation to allow healing energy to flow through the healer to the patient.
- Throughout the healing session keep checking that your feet are firmly on the ground, and keep your movements slow and deliberate, but light. Begin by working off the body, in the energy field: your hands will be about 10–15 centimetres (4–6 inches) away from the physical body.
- Hold both hands over the crown of your patient's head. You will probably feel a tingling as you enter the energy field and you may be aware of a flow through your hands into the patient's crown chakra – but don't worry if you feel nothing at all. Many seasoned and successful healers simply trust and know that something is happening, without any specific subtle awareness of the process.
- Move so that you are standing on the right of your patient. (This is so that your right hand can easily treat the chakra petals, and your left, the chakra stems.) Hold your right hand over the petals of the brow chakra and your left hand over the stem. Keep a sense of timing and then move on to work with your right hand over the throat chakra petals and your left at its stem. (In your early healing sessions do not treat the alter major chakra: it has a different polarity and you can add it in later. It is discussed more fully in Chapter 5.)

Healing the throat chakra.

• Move rhythmically on through the chakras, right hand over the petals and left over the stem until you reach the root chakra. This should be healed with both hands, similarly to the crown, by placing your hands over the base of the spine or by kneeling down and placing them, palms upwards, under the chair. (Throughout the healing session be aware that as energy passes though physical matter, you do not need to feel blocked by the back or seat of the chair.)

- Now, provided your patient has given permission, you are ready to begin touching the body. First, kneel at your patient's feet and hold each one in turn, with your left hand under the sole of the foot and your right hand on the upper part. Then, if your patient has any aches or pains or specific areas requiring healing, put your hands gently on or over each of these parts. As you get more confident in perceiving the energy flow let the energy dictate the length of time you stay in each place. If you are uncertain, the general rule is not more than five minutes on any one spot.

- When you have finished this specific healing, it is a good idea to 'comb' your patient's aura. You do this with the tips of your fingers, making long, sweeping strokes downwards in the auric field, working from head to feet. This helps to balance your patient's aura and also in the process of regrounding. Move all around your patient as you do this, beginning at your patient's right side and finishing off at the back.

- Rest your hands, from behind, lightly on your patient's shoulders and simply say 'thank you'. It is good to say this out loud, because it tells the patient that the healing is almost over. The final part is to stand away from your patient and make the all-important energetic separation (see page 23).

- Allow your patient time to begin to come back fully into the everyday world and, if possible, offer a cup of tea or a glass of water. As you prepare these, you might like to take the opportunity to wash your hands as a final earthing and grounding.

Energetic separation: saying 'Thank you' (see page 41).

Exercise
Healing Sequence 2, Patient Lying Down

This healing sequence is based on giving attention to the same energy centres as in the sequence described above, but it is used when your patient needs or prefers to lie down.

Often the only place to lie will be a settee or bed, where there is very limited scope for the healer to move around the patient. If there is space underneath the bed and the patient lies near one edge it may be possible to heal the petals of the chakras with one hand and the stems with the other, but on many beds or settees it is not possible to heal in this way without asking the patient to move about or change position rather often.

In general it is best if the healing session is quiet, peaceful or almost meditative. Asking the patient to lie first one way and then another, even if they are well enough to do so, is disruptive to both healer and patient. Try to have some reasonably free access to the patient's head. (If they are not actually ill in bed, lying with the head at the foot of the bed or diagonally across a large bed can be a good way of accomplishing this. It might also be possible to organise a makeshift bed or mattress on the floor so that the healer, kneeling or sitting, can have full access from every angle.)

The patient should lie on their back, with a pillow under the knees for comfort and support if necessary. Or you can heal the front first and if it is comfortable for the patient, they can turn over halfway through the session. Alternatively, you might ask the patient to lie on one side. Eventually, if only one position is possible and access limited, heal where you can and trust that the healing energy will go to wherever it is needed most.

If kneeling is uncomfortable for you, as the healer, or you feel it to be ungainly in any way, it is best to either stand or sit on a low stool near the patient and to try to position yourself so that your back can be as straight as possible.

- Once your patient is comfortable and you have decided whether to kneel, stand or sit for the actual healing, stand up to do your grounding and running energy preparation (see page 20). Then, if possible, sit, stand or kneel behind your patient's head and gently focus on the crown chakra, using both hands in the energy field, as described in the first healing exercise (see page 18).
- As you work on the rest of the energy points, you can either use both hands over each, or you may prefer to

put your left hand on your left knee (with your foot flat on the ground) and work only with your right hand. The left hand on your left knee acts as grounding energy for you, as the healer, and allows anything that the patient may need to release to go into the earth.

- In this way, either using both hands together or keeping your left hand on your left knee and holding your right hand in the energy field over each chakra, work progressively through the chakras – crown, brow, throat, heart, solar plexus, sacral and root. At the root, working in the energy field, the position for your right hand is roughly over the pubic bone. If you are able to use your left hand at the same time, its best position for healing the root chakra is over the coccyx.

Healing a patient who is lying down.

- Now, if you can, place your right hand on or over the patient's left foot and your left hand on or over the right foot. After this, place your hands on or over any area where there is pain or where specific healing may have been asked for.

- Comb your patient's aura (see page 40) and then rest
  your hands either on your patient's shoulders or place
  them together under and cradling their head. As you
  bring the session to an end, say 'thank you', move away
  from the bed or couch, and make the energetic
  separation (see page 23). Allow yourself and your patient
  a few moments of silence before resuming normal
  conversation or having a cup of tea or some water
  together.

You have now built on the sequence that established a
healing flow (see page 25) and begun to use the chakra
energy centres for focusing the healing you invoke and
channel. As you become more experienced, you may feel
naturally drawn to holding your hands in other positions.
Trust your intuition if this happens. These healing sequences
are intended to get you started, not to be slavishly followed
at all times. Throughout the book there will be suggestions
for different healing sequences and for elements that you
can add to the basic pattern. It is important for you, as a
healer, to have individuality and confidence in your work.

After a while you may become more sensitive to energies,
although do not worry if you rarely feel anything. You can
train your energetic awareness and it grows naturally with
experience, but always remember that some very experienced healers continue to feel little other than a sense of
connection and a belief that they are instrumental in channelling healing energy. At some point, your patients are
bound to ask you what you have felt or sensed and may
expect you to be able to say what your sensing means. If you
are not a natural 'senser' you can always turn the question
around and ask what the patient's experience has been. The
next chapter includes reference to sensations you or your
patients may become aware of energetically during a healing
session and how to interpret this sort of information.

Chapter 3

Healing in Practice

*Mark's story – How healers are perceived – Tempering patients'
expectations – Using invocations – The healing intent – Planning
and managing a healing session – Sensations to be expected
during healing – Using your intuition – Diagnosing illness –
Exercises – Structuring your healing session*

Allowing yourself to become known as someone who can
give healing, even if only with family and close friends, can
cause reactions in yourself and others that need addressing
quite early on.

MARK'S STORY

Mark's experience was similar to Stella's (see page 11) but in
some ways entirely different. Mark's family also realised
early on in his life that he had a talent for soothing pain and
distress. His gift was first noticed in connection with animals.
He was a tender-hearted child, particularly interested in
nature. The family cat, Bella, had always had a special affin-
ity with Mark, but one evening she came home with deep

gashes, probably from barbed wire, and had to have her wounds stitched. She was in pain, fighting infection and began to refuse food. She lay curled up miserably in her bed, growing weak and thin, and not recovering well.

Mark was the only family member who could get a response from her or bring her any apparent comfort. He would sit beside her quietly and then, without touching her sensitive body, gently make rhythmic stroking movements. This calmed the cat and she began to accept food again, first from Mark's hand and then quite soon finding the strength to get up and eat from her bowl. In a remarkably short time, from apparently having given up on life, the cat was well again, had her stitches out and never looked back, living on to a ripe old age.

Mark's parents felt great awe at his obvious healing effect on Bella. They were excited by what they saw as a special potential and giftedness in their son. They began to treat him differently, almost reverently, and told all their friends the story of Bella. It was not long before Mark was asked if he could help to heal a friend's dog. When this was a success too, he often found himself in demand when friends' and family's animals were injured or 'off colour'. Of course, it was not long before he was asked to give some healing to an aunt with migraine, an uncle with asthma and a neighbour's child with earache.

At first Mark enjoyed the attention and the novelty of sharing his new-found skill, but gradually he began to feel that he would rather be out playing with his friends, racing his model cars or watching television. He was a normal, fun-loving child, but his parents became quite obsessed with his gifts and began to overprotect him and make him different from other children. He felt that his childhood was truncated from the moment he helped Bella the cat, and his relationship to his parents changed. He felt driven into an early rebellion against all things parental in order to claim an ordinary life for himself. He said: 'I really believe something was getting quite out of hand and that if my parents had been religious they could have started some kind of cult, with me and my healing as the focus for it.'

As it was, Mark's parents didn't really know what to do about his gift. They felt he had special powers, but could hardly send a ten-year-old child to be trained as a healer. They did try to encourage him to study medicine or nursing, but Mark had been convinced from an early age that he really wanted to become an architect. When I got to know him, he had achieved that ambition. He was in the process of rebuilding the relationship with his parents that had broken down as a result of his rebellion and his leaving for a university as far away from home as possible at the earliest moment.

Although Mark had wanted to put distance between himself and healing and all that it had stirred up for him, he would never be totally mundane in his outlook and philosophies. He had cared for his spiritual side by becoming interested in transpersonal psychology (see Glossary, page 194) and doing a number of workshops. As he said, 'I know that I do have healing gifts and I don't want to abandon them completely, though because of that early experience I feel quite dismayed by the archetype of healing.'

HOW HEALERS ARE PERCEIVED

Archetypes affect us, personally and collectively, at almost every moment of our lives. By dictionary definition they are 'primordial images inherited by all'. Each human society is affected by forces such as peace, war, beauty, justice, wisdom, healing, death, birth, love and power. The essence of these forces defies definition and we need images, myths, symbols and personifications to help us in understanding the depth and breadth of them. Tarot cards, which have ancient origins, have twenty-two personified or symbolised archetypes in the major arcana. These cover most aspects of human experience.

The archetype of healing, or the healer, is powerful indeed, and all who practise healing of any kind need to be aware of that power. When a profession, calling, or activity is under the influence of a powerful archetype, it is necessary to be in the right relationship to it. If we use archetypal energies well, they can help us and even, to some extent, protect us. Yet we need to be using the archetype – rather than be used by it. If our own relationship to the archetype is comfortable, then we can help others to be comfortable with it too.

Mark had good reason to feel some dismay about the archetype of healing. When his healing gifts became manifest, the influence of the archetype had affected and confused his parents. Mark's childhood and his bond with his parents had been stressed as a result. He knew that he needed to know more about the archetype of the healer before he could comfortably engage with his healing gifts again.

TEMPERING PATIENTS' EXPECTATIONS

'Hands-on' or energetic healing is seen as a complementary therapy that aids the whole healing process. Some people fear healing or are superstitious about it, seeing it as being related to magic. Others expect it to produce miracles.

Healers in professional practice usually have a high proportion of patients who have tried everything in their search for health or a cure and who come to healing as a last resort, desperately hoping that it will achieve a cure where all else has failed. The healing movement in our society is growing, and there is no doubt that healing can and does produce astonishing results some of the time, but not all of the time. However, there will always be those particularly outstanding healers who consistently produce extraordinary outcomes to their healing interventions and whose lives are completely re-routed as a result of the many and constant demands on them. Even when healing doesn't result in a cure, it almost invariably brings a sense of peace and relaxation, a changed perspective on disease and a more positive relationship to the overall healing process.

What is expected from healing gets projected on to the healer. It only takes one or two publicised cases of uncommon results for a healer to become overwhelmed by public demand and for something akin to legend and myth to grow up around them. This is the archetype of healing at work. Once a healer is recommended to others by someone who has benefited from healing treatment, the energy can build. People begin to feel better because they have got a phone number and are going to make an appointment.

This is quite a weight for a healer to carry. Mark's (see page 46) parents were bewildered and overawed by the whole phenomenon and, quite simply, got it wrong. As a child, Mark was vulnerable and he was swept along by something that no one around him could understand. Thus he had become wary of the archetype of healing. As an adult healer, he knew that he needed to be in a position to explain his own vision of healing fully to potential clients and to help them to an understanding of what to expect from it – and from him.

The ability to do this applies to the non-professional healer, working mainly with family and friends, as much as to the professional. Too much build-up of expectation on the part of either the healer or the client will inevitably lead to disappointment or disillusionment. Seeing the movement from disease to health and well-being as a journey that the healer can support and accompany is one way of ensuring that the archetype is being used rather than being allowed to take control.

Explaining that healing can help you to help yourself, or your self-healing mechanism to re-start itself, prevents patients from expecting instant results or from abdicating their own responsibilities on the healing quest. The majority of healings are not phenomena from another dimension, but the result of co-operative work between healer and client, usually as a complement to other therapies.

As a healer, you experience the urge to heal. Both you and your patients will want to fit this experience into some sort of belief system or structure. If you heal, you will ask and be asked questions about it, such as how you discovered you had the ability or inclination to heal, whether you do it as part of a religious faith or belief, whether you believe in miracles, whether healing drains you in any way, and what you feel, sense, see and know when you are in the process of giving healing.

You may have a specific religious faith or belief. You may consider yourself to be on a spiritual path, or feel that because you can heal you need to find one. You may come from a humanist perspective. Whatever the framework, most healers regard themselves as channels or instruments for healing energy. Whether you take the most basic image for healing, in which the healer is like the jump leads coming from a healthy car battery to one that is run down and needs charging, or prefer to describe the healing force as a universal energy or healing flow, without linking it to a religious or spiritual source, you will need to align yourself with the healing energy.

The grounding and running energy exercise (see page 20) is also an alignment exercise, and adding an affirmation or invocation will help you to focus on your healing, your patient, your healing purpose and intent, as well as to become clearer about your healing role. All this will help when you are planning and managing your healing sessions.

USING INVOCATIONS

A good way of getting clarity of intention in healing is to make use of invocation, which is described in *Chambers 20th Century Dictionary* as 'the act or the form of invoking or addressing in prayer or supplication: an appellation under which one is invoked: any formal invoking of the blessing or help of a god, a saint, etc.: an opening prayer in a public religious service or in the Litany: a call for inspiration from a Muse or other deity as at the beginning of a poem: an incantation or calling up of a spirit: a call or summons.'

Your invocation may be very brief or more complex and poetic. It is important that you feel comfortable with the wording and content of your invocation. As a non-professional healer you will probably know the people to whom you offer healing reasonably well and may want to say your invocation out loud, thus involving your patient in this part of the preparation, or you may prefer to make your invocation silently.

The invocation can be placed at the very beginning of your healing preparation, before you do the grounding exercise, or you may make it afterwards, as you step towards your patient and begin the actual healing sequence or interaction.

If you believe in angels or like the idea of angelic qualities as blessing and support for your healing, you can name them very simply as part of the words of your invocation. My book, *Working with Guides and Angels*, will give you more information about angels and about invocation (see Further Reading, page 195). If you have a specific religion, you will probably use a form of prayer that you know to be appropriate to your healing invocation and intent. Here are a few simple suggestions for invocations that might be used by anyone as a support to the healing preparation:

- I align myself with the power of healing.
- I invoke healing energy.

- I offer myself as an instrument for enabling healing.
- I invoke the angels of love, light and healing.
- May I be used as a channel for grace.
- May we be receptive to the energy of healing.
- Thank you for the power/grace of healing.
- Let me be a clear channel for true healing.
- Let this healing be used according to the need of the patient.

Simple sentences are best, but if you want to put several together to make something more rounded or poetic, use the creation of your own favourite invocation(s) as a means of becoming more explicit with yourself about how you view the healing energy and your role as a healer.

One suggestion for combining some of the sentences above would be:

> I invoke the angels of light and love and healing. I align myself with the power of healing in order to be used as a channel for grace. May I be receptive to the healing force and channel it with love.

When training healers, I always ask them to make a collection of invocations, some created by themselves and others gathered or extracted from other sources. Such an exercise helps greatly in defining and developing your ability to speak about healing and what it means to you.

THE HEALING INTENT

It may seem that healing intent can be defined quite simply as the intention to heal the patient of whatever is ailing them. Earlier I suggested that the main purpose of energetic healing is to kickstart the patient's own self-healing mechanisms and to give support whilst or until this happens.

It is important for the healer to be clear about intent, both as part of relating to the archetype of healing, and also because thinking deeply about healing invocation and intent is part of the necessary process of forming a philosophy of healing. This is discussed in greater detail in Chapter 4, but I feel it is important to say that too much focus on specifics and symptoms in the healing intent can be limiting to both healer and patient.

Obviously if a patient has a broken leg, you will both have it within your intent to use the healing to help the bone to knit and any pain and discomfort to be minimised. Yet even in such a straightforward situation as this, it is necessary to include in the intent a general healing for the patient and where they happen to be in life at the moment, as well as a specific healing for the broken leg and the pain.

Even a broken leg or other accidental injury can be a symptom. What caused the accident, both directly and in-directly? What emotional as well as physical upset and frustration is the patient suffering as a result of the accident and the incapacity? What contributed to making this acci-dent happen at this time? Any injury or illness, however seemingly accidental or haphazard, is a part of the whole, wider picture and the healing intent needs to be both clear and open.

If a healer is too attached to achieving specific results or to working with the symptomatic manifestation of illness or accident, something wider may be missed. As an everyday healer, you may protest that you only want to use a natural gift to be of help, so why make it more complex? – and actu-ally this is right. Wanting to use a natural gift in order to be of help is an ideal intent, being simple, clear and yet open.

If you want to expand your knowledge of how healing works and of the symbolism of healing and disease, it is wise to keep in mind the basic, simple premise with which you set out. Even if you go on to develop other skills to help where the journey to healing seems blocked, try to retain a simplicity of approach and intent, but one which widens, rather than narrows, the framework within which you work. As you work with invocation and intent, let each of them reflect something of this simplicity and directness.

PLANNING AND MANAGING A HEALING SESSION

Gradually, a healing session will come to include much more than having a patient ask or come for healing, arranging them on a chair, bed or couch and conducting a healing session. Giving thought to invocation and intent will enable you to express your thoughts about healing more clearly and therefore to plan and manage a full healing session.

When planning a healing session, you need to remember that your patient may never have received healing before and may not know what to expect. It is up to you to put people at ease by explaining clearly but simply what healing is and describing briefly what you intend to do during the healing session. It is a good idea to write yourself a script – not, of course, to read from when greeting your patient, but so that you can see everything clearly thought out and written down, and know the words you intend or are likely to use.

Your patient, even if already well known to you, will almost certainly want to describe the history of their complaint and reasons for seeking healing. After listening to this, you will probably want to ask what expectations your patient has of the treatment with you. At a first visit or healing interaction, it is also a good idea to be clear about whether this is a 'one-off' healing, or whether you are going to meet regularly for a while and then have an interim assessment of how things are going. If you have an ongoing or more long-term client, it is always a good idea to build in points of review, say after every four or six sessions, so that each of you can decide about commitment to further sessions. (Frequency of healing sessions is discussed in Chapter 7.)

If you have, or choose to develop, skills that are complementary to healing, such as counselling, you will probably want to get more involved with the emotional and symbolic aspects of illness and spend time exploring these aspects with your patient.

Every healing session may have a different format from the last. You may intuitively use a different order of events or format for different patients, but on the whole your patient will want to know how long the session is likely to last, and there are certain standard procedures you need to incorporate. On page 58 there is a checklist for session management, including rounding off, and completing the energetic separation by tidying and perhaps cleansing the space at the end of the session.

Preparing the Healing Space

It is ideal, of course, if you can set aside a separate room or contained space for your healings, but this will probably be difficult unless you eventually decide to heal as a professional. If you are fortunate enough to have a separate space, you need to keep it physically and psychically clean and clear, because healing has a subtle and sacred aspect to it.

Try to have colour in the space, usually light, bright, pastel colours. Blues, pinks, greens and yellows are all good (see the section on colour in Chapter 5). If you are adapting a normal living space, a blanket, cloth for a table, cushion or so, flowers, plants, crystals and/or candles in these colours will help you to make the space more special.

Try to have two chairs of similar sitting height for you and your patient to sit on for the times when you will be talking together. You will also need cushions for feet, head or to put under the knees of patients who may lie down on a couch or the floor. Rugs or light blankets should be on hand for covering and warmth, together with socks if the patient wants to remove their shoes. It is a good idea to have a jug and two glasses for drinking water, and a bowl of water and small towel in which you can wash your hands before you begin the healing intervention and at its end.

Cleansing the healing space

In preparation for healing your patient, the space can be psychically cleansed in several ways. You can use:

Sound Music (Baroque is excellent); a shamanic rattle, singing bowl or rainstick (see Chapter 7).

Fragrance A fragranced candle or an oil burner. Use this before your patient arrives and put out the heat source for the oil before you begin the healing as you do not want any fragrance to be too powerful during the actual healing session (see Chapter 7).

Smudge sticks These are bunches of herbs that you light and then put out so that they are smouldering. You waft the resulting fragrance and smoke around the room and objects in the room to psychically cleanse and clear them. Smudging is a good way of attending to corners where negative energy residues may collect.

Prayer and invocation As you prepare for your patient, you might say your favourite prayer or invocation in the room or space, silently or aloud.

Attention to and preparation of your healing space is also preparation for yourself. Allow time for it and do it carefully. When your patient has left the space, you may also want to repeat some of the psychic cleansing above, either in preparation for a new patient, or in order to establish a boundary between healing space and normal living space.

Session Management Checklist

This checklist will help you manage your healing sessions. When you are still at the practise stage, you may feel it is a little too formal – but it is best to be systematic right from the start. Even though you might miss out some elements in certain informal situations, try to incorporate a sense of ritual and thorough readiness at all times, out of respect both for the power of healing and for yourself and your patients.

Decide how long you need for a healing session. The shortest healing session usually lasts about twenty minutes. In addition, you need time for preparation, time for greeting and talking with your patient, and time for rounding off at the end. Never expect a patient to go too quickly from receiving healing to everyday activities and encourage them to make sure that they don't have to get straight up from the healing space in order to drive a car, catch a bus, collect a child from school, etc.

1. Prepare your space Make sure it is physically clean and tidy; gather your props (including blankets, pillows and socks, as well as tea and water); and cleanse it psychically (see page 57).

2. Prepare yourself Before the patient arrives, say your invocation (see page 52) and do your grounding and running energy exercise (see page 20).

3. Greet your patient Know where you will put coats, whether or not you will ask that shoes are removed; offer refreshments (tea or water).

4. Talk with your patient Ask what they may be expecting, and give an opportunity for any questions to be asked.

- Give information about how you conduct the healing session and ask your patient any questions you consider appropriate about their reasons for coming for healing.
- Explain that you will probably be silent during the healing session but encourage your patient to know that it is all right to speak, move and react to the healing.
- Explain that extra pillows or coverings are available and that you will want to know if your patient feels uncomfortable in any way, including about anything you do during the healing that the patient may want to question you about.
- Be clear about whether or not your patient is happy with being touched at the appropriate time in the healing intervention.

5. Place your patient ready for the healing session Reground yourself, maybe teaching this exercise to your patient as well (see page 20); remind yourself of your healing intent and/or invocation (see page 52).

6. Carry out the healing exercise of your choice.

7. Do the energetic separation (see page 23).

8. After a little time, ask your patient to move from the healing chair or couch, offer more water or tea and exchange what each of you has experienced during the session.

9. Make any arrangements that need to be made about future sessions. Make sure that your patient can contact you if they are worried about anything in the interim. Make sure that your patient has gathered all personal belongings. End the session.

10. Rearrange your room, play music, or generally cleanse

the space as you did before interacting with your patient, leaving it ready for your next patient or for its normal use.

SENSATIONS TO BE EXPECTED DURING HEALING

As you practise the healing exercises suggested so far, you will begin to feel or perceive things that are happening for you and your patient in terms of energy flow. Gradually you will respond to certain perceptions of what is going on. Where energy is experienced as 'fizzy', you will bring in the intention to quieten and calm. As well as an overall healing intention for your patient you will have intentions of the moment, which develop in response to what you are sensing.

Knowing the meanings of the things you begin to feel or perceive as you are giving healing is something that can only come from experience, which takes time to build and is aided by working with different patients and their different presenting symptoms.

Right from the start, it can help to have a 'vocabulary for healing' list in mind, so that you know what you might be looking for and what the energy you are channelling might be seeking to rectify. Having such a list may seem like the beginning of crossing the boundary from complete sim-plicity to greater complexity but, as you seek to be more conscious as a healer, some movement from innocent trust to increased knowledge and deliberation has to be made. My hope for healers is that moving into greater awareness will eventually help them to return to a style that is relatively unadorned and might be described as 'informed simplicity'.

The Vocabulary of Healing

Here is the vocabulary for healing list (in alphabetical order):

agitated, alive, asleep, awake, balanced, blocked,

blossoming, bold, bright, brittle, bubbly, budding, calm, changeable, closed, cool, cold, collected, complex, composed, consistent, dark, dead, difficult, distressed, dry, dull, easy, empty, excited, effervescent, electrical, faint, fast, fertile, fiery, floppy, flowing, free, full, gentle, gritty, grounded, growing, hard, harsh, healthy, heavy, hot, hungry, icy, immobile, inconsistent, insubstantial, irregular, jarring, joyful, jumpy, light, lively, magnetic, moist, moving, narrow, normal, nourished, open, peaceful, prickly, pulsating, quick, quickening, quiet, receptive, regular, released, replete, resistant, restful, restorative, rigid, sad, scattered, sensitive, simple, slow, smooth, soft, solid, spiky, stable, stagnant, static, steady, sticky, stiff, strong, stuck, substantial, sustained, tingling, thick, thirsty, unbalanced, undernourished, ungrounded, unreceptive, unstable, unsteady, unsustained, warm, weak, wide.

These words all describe ways of perceiving how the energy in chakras, aura and body may be manifesting. The list is not totally comprehensive, and you may want to add words of your own, but it is a starting point.

Words Describing Healthy Energies

Obviously, healthy energies will tend to be perceived as:

alive, awake, balanced, blossoming, bright, calm, collected, composed, consistent, easy, electrical, fertile, flowing, free, gentle, grounded, healthy, joyful, light, lively, magnetic, moving, normal, nourished, peaceful, quiet, receptive, regular, restful, restorative, stable, smooth, steady, sustained.

Words Describing Energies That Need Attention

Energies that are out of balance or needing attention of some kind may be perceived as:

agitated, bold, brittle, bubbly, budding, changeable,
closed, cool, cold, complex, dead, difficult, distressed,
dry, dull, empty, excited, effervescent, faint, fast, fiery,
floppy, gritty, growing, hard, harsh, heavy, hot, hungry,
icy, immobile, inconsistent, insubstantial, irregular,
jarring, jumpy, moist, narrow, open, prickly, pulsating,
quick, quickening, released, replete, resistant, rigid, sad,
scattered, sensitive, simple, slow, soft, solid, spiky,
stagnant, static, sticky, stiff, strong, stuck, substantial,
tingling, thick, thirsty, unbalanced, undernourished,
ungrounded, unreceptive, unstable, unsteady,
unsustained, warm, weak, wide.

Sensing the Meanings of Different Energies

It will be largely self-evident that agitated energy needs
calming, changeable energy needs steadying, cold areas
need warming, dead ones enlivening and hungry ones
feeding, but there are also words in the list that may or may
not indicate the need for change. If certain kinds of energy
are perceived, the healer needs to sense further and maybe
ask inner questions.

Overall, balance is what a healer is aiming to achieve or
has as an intention. Thus, a bold energy can be positive, or
it could be too bold and out of proportion to other energies
that may be perceived. A bubbly energy might feel balanced
and productive, recuperative and responsive or it might
be unbalanced. Where there is emptiness, there might be
deadness, but there could also be a sense of clearance and
anticipation. A perception of fullness might indicate near
blockage, or might be the fullness that precedes blossoming.
Effervescent energy can indicate life returning to an area
that needs to be encouraged, but can also mean overactivity that needs to be quietened. An open energy may
mean that something has been satisfactorily released, but if
chakras, in particular, are too open, depletion and exhaus-
tion may be present in the patient. Similarly, a closed energy

may mean that there is a healthy protection, but could signal resistance or a potential underlying blockage. Whatever you sense, you need also to consider its relationship to the environment, yourself and your patient's condition. Your intuition is always your best guide and will naturally strengthen as you gain experience in healing.

Familiarising yourself with these words, or choosing a few from the list to have in mind when healing, will give you a vocabulary for what you may perceive, and help you to be more informed about what is happening when you heal. It may also enable you to be aware of areas that need more focus during the healing intervention. As your experience builds and your perceptions heighten, your sensing of what is going on will tell you more and more about the needs of your patient and enable your healing responses to be more specific.

USING YOUR INTUITION

As you begin to notice what needs to be achieved energetically for your patient, you may intuitively begin to develop some particular hand gestures, or decide you want to use crystals, fragrances or colours as aids to your healing sequence (see Chapter 7). When you are healing, your hands will usually be relaxed and slightly curved, with fingers together but not rigidly so, but you may now find that you are drawn to use only your fingers, only some of your fingers or mainly the palms of your hands. Trust this. Where you can, practise and experiment with like-minded friends who will give you feedback, or look for a group of healers to join, where such things can be discussed. You may also decide that you don't want to do anything more than hold your hands over certain areas with the aim of achieving balance. Some people move their hands rhythmically, others keep them still – use your intuition.

The middle pathway between a relatively complex healing procedure and a very simple one is to note what seems to be happening in the patient's energy field and to know by intent what you want to accomplish. Focusing this intention into specific areas will bring a natural direction to your healing and will be something to discuss with your patient after the healing has taken place and before further healing is given.

Involving your patient in the healing process is important. If you discuss what you have sensed and make suggestions for what needs to be achieved, your patient can hold this in mind between sessions and use it for meditative self-healing. (This is further discussed in Chapters 4 and 7.)

DIAGNOSING ILLNESSES

There are gifted, sensitive, mediumistic or clairvoyant healers who can diagnose physical illnesses without recourse to medical science but, apart from knowing what is happening in the energy field and chakras, even professional healers are well advised to leave specific diagnosis aside. As your sensitivity develops, you may pick up on organs in the body that do not seem to be functioning well or that you suspect are diseased.

Such sensings need to be reported gently to your patient, without creating alarm, and with the advice to visit a doctor to get things checked out. If you sense 'stuck' energy in the liver, for example, it does not necessarily mean that the organ is diseased, but healing is best practised as a complementary therapy, not an alternative one: when in doubt, both you and your patient may need expert advice. Also bear in mind that no one's energy field is perfectly balanced. There will be 'blocks' but most of these are fairly harmless. As you do more healing you will begin to sense when someone is 'ill'.

Rapport between doctors and healers can sometimes be fraught with difficulty. Doctors have legal obligations to their patients. Healers can be woefully lacking in tact and respect when it comes to imparting what they sense or intuit. It is well to remember that the majority of doctors enter the profession because they are dedicated to the healing of disease. They undergo many years of training and have sophisticated tools available for making diagnoses.

As healers, we may feel that medical science is too symptom orientated and not in touch with the healing of the whole person, or fails to give enough weight to what the individual may choose in the way of treatment. Thankfully, this is gradually changing and doctors' patients are given more information and choice. Many surgeries now invite healers to work with those patients who are open to it.

Co-operation between the medical profession and complementary therapies progresses where there is mutual respect. To aid this, it is best if most healers focus on energy imbalances and leave scientific diagnosis to those who are best trained and equipped to attempt it. Chapter 4 explains something of the deeper, symbolic level of symptoms. (Appendix B, see page 189, gives a list of symptoms that should be reported to a doctor, if they have not already been, before progressing further with the healing.)

STRUCTURING YOUR HEALING SESSION

Now you can begin to expand your basic healing technique with these simple steps.

Step 1 Invocations

Write some invocations that you can use as part of your preparation to heal (see page 52).

Step 2 Statement of Intent

Write out a statement of general intent for yourself as a
healer and as a focus for your healing sessions (see page 53).

Step 3 Healing Sequences

Practise the healing sequences on pages 25, 39 and 42, but
select some words from the list on page 60 as an aid to developing your awareness of what is happening and adjusting
your input into the healing session.

For instance, you might select 'agitated', 'cold' and 'resistant', and endeavour to sense any instances of this in your
patient's energy field. If you find an agitated area, practise
calming or soothing it; warm a cold area and ease a resistant
area into flow. Use your hands naturally and intuitively and
'think' the changes you have an intention to make.

This chapter has been intended to help you to think more
deeply about the implications of being a healer, develop
your healing perceptions and responses, and manage a
healing session in detail. In the next chapter we shall be
looking at healing as a philosophy and process, and at the
symbolic meaning of illness.

Chapter 4

The Meaning of Disease

Finding our true selves – The symbolic meanings of symptoms –
Joshua's story – Exploring symptoms as symbols – Breakdown to
breakthrough – Chloe's story – Exercise

My guide, Gildas, teaches that Earth is the only planet on which part of our learning and evolution takes place through disease. The process of healing should therefore be seen as a journey to new insight and maturity, rather than as a return to a state of health previously known. Disease and symptoms are communications from our bodies on behalf of the whole of our psyche or being. Learning and striving to be well stretches us physically, but also emotionally, mentally and spiritually.

Illness has symbolic meaning. If the word 'disease' is split, it becomes 'dis-ease'. This is the state that often precedes illness and can be spiritual, emotional, physical or mental in origin.

We should take seriously those times when we are uneasy in our lives or bodies. The expectations imposed on us, both by others and by ourselves, may cause us stress. The tendency is to 'give ourselves a good talking to', take a deep breath, call on our willpower and then carry on with the same old patterns. We too easily forget that such 'dis-ease' can eventually produce more chronic ill-health and sickness.

'Mind over matter' is an attitude to life that is often greatly admired but frequently misunderstood. We endeavour to subjugate body and emotions to the discipline and directions of our minds. We are conditioned to, or filled with, expectations of what we 'ought' to be. Parents, teachers and society have an investment in moulding or forcing us into conformity. We are pressured into pursuing interests seen by others as being 'good' for us. We must perform to a preset standard and generally become 'happy', 'normal', or 'well adjusted'. Our minds learn to believe that these norms or expectations are right. We may turn ourselves inside out in order to please others and fulfil their ambitions for us. We desperately yearn for approval.

Finding Our True Selves

A gardener who decides to plant some unlabelled but interesting-looking seeds will watch their growth carefully, assessing their needs as they grow. He will be interested to observe their progress and see what sort of plant each is becoming. Should there be flower or fruit, he will be delighted with the result. Whatever the shape, colour or size, he will be content if each plant is healthy and flourishing. He will let those that want to grow tall have support. He will see that the shorter, bushier ones have enough light and ground space.

A gardener knows that a seed holds a certain blueprint or potential. It is useless to plant a tomato seed if you want to grow an oak tree; no amount of persuasion, tending, discipline or threat will make the seed change. If the conditions are not right for the seed, it will sicken and die.

Of course, the analogy between a seed and a human being

cannot be pushed too far, but nevertheless it serves to set us thinking about the nature of disease. However much we may struggle to gain approval and to be what others ask of us, our feelings and emotions will eventually make it clear if we are a 'square peg in a round hole'.

If feelings are ignored and the mind pushes us on, or entrenches us further in areas where we cannot express the true self, the body will begin to collude. It will become the servant of our emotions, because when the body fails, life change may be forced upon us. When we learn to listen both to our emotions and to our bodies, and understand the messages we are being given, then we may be able to choose change before change chooses us.

It is more difficult to avoid the signals of the body than of the mind. If the body is ill, we cannot continue. If we ignore the messages of minor symptoms, they may develop into something more major or we may have an accident.

Pain is an example here. It is nature's way of signalling when something is wrong. If we merely kill the pain with pills in order to carry on our lifestyle without interruptions, we may be choosing to ignore an important message and be in danger of leaving the real meaning behind the cause of our trouble undetected and untreated. If we do not examine our life pattern, a serious illness or breakdown may develop. Recurring headaches can develop into heart attacks or strokes. Life-threatening illnesses, forcing us to consider our quality of life, can develop from symptoms we choose to ignore.

Even when we attend to our symptoms, getting rid of them is not necessarily the way to true, whole health. In order to heal ourselves deeply, rather than merely being satisfied with removing symptoms, we may need to understand what they are telling us and be prepared to make such life changes as allow the true self to shine through. If we listen to symptoms in depth and at an early stage, we may not need to become seriously ill in order to shift the pattern.

Symptoms can be ambassadors on behalf of our emotions and our true selves.

THE SYMBOLIC MEANINGS OF SYMPTOMS

Instead of seeing disease as an attacker or a monster on the path, we should consider the symbolic wisdom which it encompasses. Symptoms certainly carry warnings in the early stages. They are potential friends or allies, and every symptom bears a different message. Although there may be a common thread in the message carried by a particular group of symptoms, the total communication to the individual manifesting such symptoms is unique and personal.

Lists suggesting symbolic meanings for symptoms should be used only as a guide to further personal insight. Many books give blanket indications of what dis-ease means for an individual; of emotional sources of dis-ease. Such information can be misleading, since the sources of a dis-ease can vary from person to person – for instance, while breast cancer may often indicate an over-attachment to family, this is not necessarily the case.

To be told that trouble with your gall bladder means you are unconsciously bitter may bring insight to some, but guilt and self-recrimination to others. As healers who may discuss the symbolic meaning of disease with our patients, we must take great care not to add a burden of guilt to the already existing burden of illness.

Bitterness (because of the gall) must certainly be considered by those with weakness in this area, but it is possible to open the exploration more gently. A less accusatory, categorical or judgemental approach would be to ask: 'What is the bitter pill that life has presented me with and caused me to swallow? Must I continue to swallow it? Are there any life and/or attitudinal changes I might make that would be to my advantage?'

There is an attitude to self-responsibility in alternative and complementary medicine circles that can all too easily add the burden of guilt to that of disease. Interpreting illness symbolically should not be a way of saying: 'It's really all your fault. You've done this to yourself, so what are you going to do about it now?' Rather, the exploration of symptoms as symbols should be exciting, a piece of detective work enabling each symbol to be explored as a key to greater knowledge of how the potential of the true self might be discovered and released.

An exploration of the exact expression of the many symptoms that we, as humans, can manifest is beyond the scope of this book. But we can learn how to listen to symptoms as symbols and so aid our healing process. The points to remember are:

1. Disease and symptoms can be allies rather than enemies, telling us to look at our lifestyles and to perhaps open up more. As such, they can be a path for learning and self-empowerment. See also page 78.
2. There is often a greater wisdom within the sick-self than in the conditioned well-self.
3. Symptoms are signals from the sick-self that all is not well, not only physically but emotionally and perhaps spiritually too.

It behoves us to look further at the concept of the parts of ourselves that manifest as 'conditioned well-self', 'sick-self' and 'true well-self'.

The Conditioned Well-self

Our longing for approval is one of the strongest of human urges. It places a powerful weapon in the hands of those who wield authority. The child's longing for approval invests parents or teachers with the power to fashion the basic mores and social graces that enable family and community life to run smoothly. This is necessary. All can be well if that authority is tempered with wisdom and love, but that same longing for approval can create a power that is subtly corrupt. Much can go wrong if love is possessive or when there is a chain reaction of conformity based on fear, when the requirements of society have not been questioned, or when a sense of frustration causes tunnel vision.

The psychologist Carl Rogers insisted that a major requirement for successful psychotherapy is that the therapist should be able to maintain an 'unconditional positive regard' for the patient. This does not mean that the patient will not be helped to behavioural changes or discernment, but that the basic human essence must be seen and valued before healthy growth can take place. Many parents and teachers would do well to remember and observe that axiom.

All too often the child gets a message of conditional love or regard. It is as if their parents are saying, 'Do what we want you to do, become what we want you to become, be the success I never was, do not question our values, make us proud of you on our terms and all will be well, for after all we only want what is best for you – and having lived longer we know what is best for you.'

This last phrase is undoubtedly reiterated with great sincerity. It should not, however, be an excuse for that lack of sensitivity which forces a developing being into an incompatible mould. Humility and insight both allow and positively support a freer choice.

These and similar influences lead us to acquire a 'conditioned well-self', which is not our true self. We sense that in some way we are gaining approval. We have chosen the right job, we have made a 'good' marriage, we have worked or are working towards a lovely home, lots of material possessions and the traditional 2.4 children. Conversely, we may feel that we are approved of because we have rejected all these values and are suitably scruffy, ill-fed, rebellious and unemployed. Peer groups take over from parents as the approving authorities and parents can project their own rebellions as well as their own conformities on to their children. In short, we only escape the conditioned well-self when we take the courage to choose for ourselves.

The Sick-self

The conditioned well-self easily gives rise to the sick-self, leading us to pursue false values and false means of gaining self-respect. Too much conformity to the conditioned well-self can lead us into mental, physical, emotional or spiritual illnesses and breakdowns. Often, such breakdowns contain wisdom and force a reassessment of our lifestyle, life values and choices. Although such hiatuses are devastating, breakdown of the conditioned well-self into the sick-self can be a means of breaking through to the true self.

Obviously it is altogether better if we can reassess the patterns when we are in a state of un-ease or dis-ease rather than having to enter full sickness or breakdown to gain awareness. Pursuing insight is not always straightforward. There are ties that bind us to negative patterns and permissions we lack that can be very powerful inhibitors indeed. Releasing the conditioned well-self in order to move on to who we truly are can be a scary business. When some 'befriending' of the sick-self takes place we may be amazed at the wisdom underlying the seeming obstacles it has been apparently intent on throwing across our life path.

We get job-weary, bored, irritable, inexplicably overtired or lose our sense of meaning. At such times we force ourselves on because we see no way of releasing conditioned values and expectations. If we force too far, the sick-self with its intrinsic underlying wisdom may step in. It is worth our while to learn to understand its language.

The True Well-self

We cannot overturn all the conditioned choices we have made – and will rarely want to. However, constant reassessment and attention to the things that truly make our hearts sing are important to the well-being and nourishment of the true well-self. When this blossoms, vitality, energy and positive all-round healthfulness are released into our lives. To enable this, we have to be more aware of the compromises we have made and be open to modifying those that no longer work for us. When the true well-self is honoured, we follow the light and purpose of our higher selves with joy as easily and naturally as a sunflower's face follows the sun.

An approach to healing that endeavours to understand the wisdom of illness can lead us to see that there is a potent natural force within each of us that urges us to release a unique and powerful potential and to transform disease into true health. Thus, disease, more broadly understood, leads us to consider our natural blueprint. It does not only have to be an obstacle on our way through life, but a guide to self-realisation.

It may seem strange to suggest that illness has benefits, yet it can be a means to getting things we lack in life, particularly before it reaches a chronic stage. As we begin to ask questions about the dynamics within illness, complex but interesting life stories emerge from the exploration. Joshua's story is an illustration of how deep the benefits of illness may lie.

JOSHUA'S STORY

Joshua came to me several times one winter for healing for sinus problems that followed the very frequent colds he was catching. Healing always seemed to help but did not prevent the problem recurring. He worked in an office where there was air conditioning. This meant that windows were rarely opened and if one person caught a cold it invariably spread. Yet as the common cold season progressed, most of the others with whom Joshua worked seemed to develop some degree of immunity and were certainly not falling prey to each and every cold brought in by visitors or staff from other departments. It seemed to Joshua that someone only had to sniff, let alone sneeze, and he would be in for the familiar syndrome: an acute cold, followed by blocked sinuses. After the first day of a cold he would usually return to work, but once the sinuses became painful he had to take time off. His work was stressful, with deadlines to meet, and having to take days off increased his problems.

When Joshua asked me to help him explore whether there were underlying reasons locking him into this miserable and recurring pattern, I asked him whether he felt there were any 'benefits' to his illness. He resisted this suggestion fairly strenuously. There were no benefits, he said, in having to take time off, miss important deadlines, build up a sickness record and suffer the recurring misery of sinus pain. Despite the stress, Joshua liked his work and would far rather meet his deadlines than spend time at home with a blocked nose and throbbing sinuses. The unwanted time off was causing him more stress at work, and he didn't see it as an unconscious desire to take time out.

Obviously we had to go deeper, so we explored what else was going on in Joshua's life and how his being ill affected his household. He had been married to Faith for three years and said that they both described their relationship as 'an inspiration'. They had met when Faith came to do some temping in Joshua's office. On leaving school, she had taken a year out and had wanted to train as a teacher, but then she had contracted glandular fever very badly. She missed most of a year of her course and decided to delay any decision about whether and when she would complete her training. Once she felt better, she had travelled abroad with a group of friends, doing casual work here and there when travel funds got low. On returning to England she had signed on with a temping agency and met Joshua when she came to give holiday cover at his office.

Joshua's childhood had not been easy. His mother died

when he was quite young and his father had been unable to cope with maintaining a secure home for Joshua, or with looking after him. This meant that he was brought up by relatives but, rather than staying with one family, was shunted around between grandparents, aunts and uncles. His father maintained as much contact as possible, and Joshua knew he cared. Although the relatives had all been kind, real mothering was something that had suddenly been cut off in his life.

Faith enjoyed home making and was good at it. Her temping meant that she could work hours that allowed her to be there for Joshua. The comfort and togetherness he enjoyed now that he was married were very precious and healing to him. He and Faith wanted a few years together before starting a family, and Faith toyed with the idea of completing her lapsed teacher training so that she could have the sort of career that blends most easily with family responsibilities. Just before the onset of Joshua's recurring sinus problems, she had applied to and been accepted at the local college.

Although Joshua applauded this in principle, and wanted to support her in her training, it seemed that there were mixed feelings in practice. Joshua knew that there would be a disruption to the comfortable routine he now enjoyed when college hours and the necessary study made their extra demands on Faith.

As a child, Joshua remembered the times when he had been ill as times of comfort. Someone would always rise to the occasion and give him the extra attention he craved. Faith, worried about this bout of ill-health that Joshua was having, had intimated that she might need to put off her return to training in order to look after him and support him until he was better.

As Joshua spoke of all this, it was as though a light bulb flashed on for him and he could see that part of him was really looking to Faith to mother him. He would never have asked her to forego or delay something he knew she had wanted to do for so long and which was part of their joint plan for the future, but his ill-health had made her offer the very thing he subconsciously wanted and had given him 'permission' to consider accepting it.

When healing Joshua, I had sensed a tightness in his heart chakra. Since colds are often more associated with the sacral and throat chakras, I had wondered about this energetic symptom. Now it was explained. His marriage had opened his heart but he was still very vulnerable from his childhood. His inner child felt threatened by the new phase that Faith's returning to college would bring about.

Since one of the standard symbolic meanings for sinus problems can be repressed or unshed tears, I asked Joshua how much he had been able to mourn for his mother. He said that one of his aunts had suggested to him that he should stay strong for his father as his father was staying strong for him, and had discouraged his natural tears and sadness. He had earned a lot of family compliments for being 'brave', but now the imminent disruption of the present status quo was tapping in to old material. He didn't feel able to ask Faith to go on mothering him – but part of him was not dealing with the potential loss of this aspect very well.

As Joshua's understanding of the emotional issues under-lying this bout of sinus infections increased, he went for some counselling sessions to help heal his inner child and release the blocked grief. When Faith understood what was happening she found a creative compromise. She had wanted to complete her training as quickly as possible, but there was an option available to do it less intensively over a longer period and she happily agreed to change to this more relaxed schedule.

The sinus problems soon began to lessen, both in frequency and intensity. Joshua continued to come for healing, to help with the process that was going on in his counselling, but he was well set to go from strength to strength.

This all took place some years ago. Faith completed her teacher training and taught for a while, until they decided to start a family. Now they have two growing children. They keep in touch with me from time to time. Joshua loves family life and Faith is doing some supply teaching with no plans to go permanent or full time. On every level they have reached a creative compromise and are able to support each other and understand the dynamics of their relationship more deeply.

EXPLORING SYMPTOMS AS SYMBOLS

Interpreting symptoms as symbols helps us to uncover yet more layers as we seek to understand the deep wisdom within disease. Our bodies speak a very simple, even primitive language. We get most from symbols when we live alongside them for a while, rather than rushing to interpret them intellectually. Symbols are rich and many-faceted, yet in another sense economical, since so much comes out of apparent simplicity. Recognising that a symbol exists starts a communication process with it, and within ourselves.

Most of us find ourselves, at some time in our lives, in a situation where we recognise that we are not totally content. We are working too many hours, in a job we do not really enjoy or that stretches us too much or not enough; we live in a town when we would rather be in the country, or vice versa; we cannot understand why those things we have always worked towards no longer seem right or comfortable.

We make excuses to delay making changes or rationalising our lifestyles. The present job must continue because it enables the children to have a better education. We are used to two holidays a year. Yes, we have a huge mortgage but it provides us with a lovely home. If I work hard now and put up with stressful conditions, I will be able to retire early. If I make changes, I might not like the new life any better than

the present one. The sacrifices I am making now are bene-
fiting others, and if I make changes they might feel let down.
I fear choice itself. It would be selfish to change. It is too late
to train or retrain. Others might be disappointed in me if I
say how unhappy I am.

In areas where we have been heavily conditioned by
parents, society or circumstances to strive for a certain
lifestyle or to achieve certain standards, our minds try to
exert willpower over emotion and even over matter. Our
emotions help us to question the old order. They encourage
us to find and live our own personal truths and values,
and to get that vital glimpse of our true selves. The body
interacts and colludes with the emotions, and produces
symptoms that make us take notice of the fact that all is not
well.

Eventually, if the symptoms are pressing enough, we may
be forced into life change. The Monday headache appears
every weekday; we have no energy to enjoy our leisure time
at the weekend and so spend it in sleep or depression; a
medical check warns us about blood pressure. If we take no
notice of the early warning systems, the daily headache can
escalate into heart attack or stroke, the weekend depression
results in us finding signs of impending serious illness.

The dramatic and life-threatening illnesses ask us the
question: 'Do you want to live or die?' Our minds and conditioning can weld us to lifestyles that sustain life but are not
about living as our true selves would have us live. In such
circumstances, the vital spark within us may be more dead
than alive.

In serious illness it is more than the actual illness symptoms themselves that court the possibility of death. Often
those symptoms have only come about because our souls are
weary and our spiritual vitality and purpose have been lost.
Part of our recovery will be to rekindle the spark and to
revise our life choices so that it burns brightly once more.

That inner spark might be called 'joy'; it produces joy and

is fed by joy. Lives that become joyless are lives where illness may issue its underlying challenge. We describe serious illnesses as life-threatening, but symbolically they might also be seen as life-seeking. They threaten the status quo but may force the changes our true selves require in order to live at all.

BREAKDOWN TO BREAKTHROUGH

The annals of healing have many stories to tell of people struck down by serious illness or accident and of the wondrous recoveries they make when their lifestyles are revised. One client discovered an aggressive cancer lump in her breast. As she recovered physically from the even more aggressive treatment required, she decided to go on the adventures in life she had always been putting on hold. Part of the build-up to her illness had been the loss of a partner. Now she realised that she could, if she so chose, be free.

She sold her assets and found simple accommodation in a warm land of her choice. Gradually she allowed herself only to make those choices that made her heart sing. In time she met and married a new partner and her present life choices come from a different place within her being than did her earlier ones. She is fit, well and full of joy. She is more healthy in body, mind and spirit than she had ever thought it possible to be. Her true self lives.

Another client, following in the family tradition of farming, became seriously affected by hay fever and allergic asthma. He suddenly revealed a heart's dream to live in town and run a good restaurant. After retraining, he was able to do this and now he has no allergic symptoms, even when he visits the family farm or gives a hand with some of the old jobs. He works hard for his dream, but his life spark has been reignited.

The body does not become ill without reason. Most of us have constitutionally vulnerable areas and produce certain types of symptom. Although familiar, these may well be urging us gradually towards major life changes or to more simple ones based on life issues we are not fully addressing but which are affecting us more than we realise. Some of the language we use about life and relationships gives us initial clues to understanding the symbolic deeper layers of our symbols:

- I can't stomach it any more; It turns my stomach; I'm having a gut reaction; It sticks in my throat; I am sick of it.
- My heart is heavy; I am sick at heart; My heart aches.
- I feel as though I have the weight of the world on my shoulders; I feel so stiff-necked; My life is rigid; It's a pain in the butt.
- I am world weary; It's doing my head in; It's getting me down.
- It irritates me; It makes me shudder; It makes me want to burst; It's a prickly/sticky situation.
- All is not well.

Such phrases are descriptive of our unease or dis-ease at a physical, emotional, mental and spiritual level. They describe how certain things in life can affect us and what they can do to us. As we express things in such a way, we may hear ourselves and decide that the way things are is not good enough and we must take steps to resolve a situation. If we listen to what we are saying about ourselves and, as a result, act to change or improve things, then the actual pain in the back, sickness or stiff neck may not manifest physically. Our language is a warning. On the other hand, if we endure too much the body can react.

Judy, a client of mine, knew that her back and neck were her most vulnerable areas. She was in a job where recent cuts had made the work she had once loved very frustrating. Her marriage was going through a tricky patch and her twins, a boy and girl aged nineteen years, were in the process of leaving home for a gap year and then university. Everything familiar was in a process of change and falling away. When she came with a really sore back and very stiff neck that was being resistant to osteopathic treatment, we worked out the following list of questions for her to ask herself:

- Am I being stiff-necked about something?
- Could I gain from being *more* stiff-necked about something? (i.e. is my body doing it for me?)
- Is something (or someone!) being a 'pain in the neck' to me?
- Am I being a pain in the neck to myself or someone else?
- Am I 'sticking my neck out' unnecessarily about some matter?
- Ought I to 'stick my neck out' more in the present situation?'
- Am I being too rigid?
- Am I being too flexible?
- Is someone on my back?
- Am I on someone else's back?
- Am I carrying too much for myself and/or others?
- Am I carrying enough? Taking enough responsibility?

Each question needs to be reversed (as above), and in the end the person exhibiting the symptoms is the only one who can give the answers. What one person experiences as stress, another may feel as positive challenge. In looking on at the lives of others, we may judge them to be under a particular pressure, but they themselves may not feel this to be so. In using symptoms as symbols to help us to see the wisdom in disease, we need to be in touch with what we feel about certain situations, rather than what we think of them.

As it was, Judy said that she could answer almost all these questions affirmatively. Work, marriage and children were all weighing on her and she on them. At one moment she would be too rigid or stiff-necked, at the next too flexible. She was carrying a great deal for others but, in a sense, not enough for herself. She realised that she had not given sufficient thought to what she really wanted as the outcome of this period of change. How would she like her own quality of living to be when she came through the various areas of transition that life was currently presenting her with?

Judy considered this and began to set some new boundaries at home and at work. She could not make immediate life changes at that point, but there were various ways in which she could ease the burden on herself. She began to see that there was opportunity as well as difficulty in whatever lay ahead, and that she could negotiate for a positive outcome to the changes that had been thrust upon her. She could take things more lightly, not feel so burdened and see hope, rather than imminent disaster, ahead.

A couple of years ago I caught a virus that left my body, particularly my legs, full of aches and pains. I lost any ease of movement and had to do everything much more slowly. I had known for some time that I was living at a very hectic pace and sometimes forcing myself to keep it up. My body was asking me to slow down. I interpreted this as quite a serious warning and have since tried to rest more, have more fun, look after my body, take more space for myself and get some of my commitments into proportion.

Looking at the language of symptoms and how we speak of life and its effects leads us to the first layers of understanding symptom as symbol, but there are even deeper areas that the symptoms our bodies produce can tell us about. Understanding symbolic body messages can result in an exploration of bodily memory and its links with our emotions. It can guide us to excise deep wounds that have been buried in the profound recesses of our beings. The body often aims to keep a flow going between unconscious and conscious, particularly where emotions and matters relating to the blossoming of the true self are concerned.

Healing our total being, with spiritual, mental and emotional aspects being taken into account in addition to the physical, necessitates the courage to be honest with ourselves and to gain deeper self-knowledge. It means seeking a deeper understanding of our interactions with the world, with relationships and with all interpersonal communication. More than this, it means learning about our intricate intrapersonal communications and the dynamics of our complex beings. Although some of these explanations are of a self-healing nature, it can be within the scope of the healer to encourage patients to make such explorations for themselves as part of the healing process.

I have quoted the following case history in my book *Chakras – A New Approach to Healing Your Life* (see Further Reading, page 195), but it shows clearly some of the deeper causes that are held within the causality of some of our ills.

CHLOE'S STORY

Chloe, an Afro-Caribbean client whose family came to live in southern England before she was one year old, wanted to explore the deeper cause of a pulled ankle tendon. The original injury had occurred two years previously whilst she and her partner were leading a group into a dance at a social gathering. The continuing pain, stiffness and weakness in her ankle were still resistant to improvement. She had explored the possibilities that she was carrying too much on behalf of others, or not being true to her inner self.

This line of questioning revealed some valuable insights, and Chloe had taken steps to make changes and redress certain balances, yet her ankle still did not heal. Medical investigation simply confirmed that the tendons had been sprained and were still weak. There was no other physical injury or apparent physical contributory cause.

Chloe's right ankle was the one affected. The right side of

the body is symbolically associated with those aspects of life demanding qualities of focus, direction, thrusting, activity, masculine principle or yang energy. The left side connects with the areas of life asking for qualities of diffuse awareness, subtlety, yielding, receptivity, feminine principle or yin energy.

Bearing this in mind, I asked Chloe whether she most often put her right, masculine, yang, leadership side forward in life, or whether she tended to function more from her feminine, yielding, receptive side?

Chloe felt that life had pushed her towards being 'up front', 'in the lead' and 'visible'. She was an attractive woman in a good partnership, but felt that in many ways the development of her truly feminine side had taken a back seat.

Chloe's family had always pushed her to do well at school. In art classes she had discovered a talent for design, but had never been allowed to enjoy it in a relaxed way. Her gift had been taken seriously and she had been expected to work hard, get top grades and go on to get a degree. She thoroughly enjoyed her present job, working with a design and display team for a large organisation, yet she often had a sense of frustration and felt that her talent had always been too developed and focused. She had never been able to indulge in it for its own sake or to dabble with all the potentials that could have been open to her.

Remarking that the injury to her ankle had occurred when she was leading others into a dance, I asked her to consider whether her right ankle might be telling her that the masculine side needed a rest and that it could be time to give the left, feminine side more chance to develop. She felt that this explanation was too simplistic and that there was something deeper and more complex involved.

I asked Chloe to close her eyes and see what image came to mind when she considered her right ankle and its injury. After a while she said she could see herself, aged about seven years old, in a Brownie uniform. The word 'tenderfoot' accompanied this image. When asked to associate to the word and the image, Chloe began to talk about a phase in her life that she had not remembered so clearly before.

As a tenderfoot Brownie, working towards full enrolment to receive the Brownie badge and become a full Brownie member, Chloe was required to do at least one good turn every day. In order to keep a check on this, Brown Owl had given each of the tenderfoot Brownies a card and some 'stick-on' stars. As good turns were done, so a star could be stuck on to the card. This was the equivalent of earning 'Brownie points'. At the end of each week, before the Brownie meeting, Chloe had to get one of her parents to sign the card to verify the number of good turns completed that week.

Chloe's parents had always required her to share tasks in the household. They told her that any good turn for her Brownie membership had to be something over and above the things she was normally expected to do. Since, as a seven-year-old, quite a lot was already demanded of her, she had difficulty in finding something extra each day that her parents would agree to mark on her card as her good turn. Indeed, if she had not done one of her usual chores to perfection, even the extra 'good turn' was not considered worthy of a star.

At the next Brownie meeting, Chloe had the least number of good turns on her record. She knew that her friends did not help in the home nearly as much as she did and was desperately upset when the Brown Owl told her that she obviously needed to try harder if she truly wanted to be an enrolled Brownie. She was unable to explain to her parents what was happening. They consistently refused to consider anything within their normal high demands of her as a good turn. Eventually, in desperation and although it cut her off from many of her friends, Chloe gave up Brownies and the tenderfoot requirements. Her parents then criticised her for lack of commitment and consistency.

As this painful memory surfaced, Chloe realised that there were similar factors operating in her current situation. Although she loved her work, knew she was good at it and often willingly worked unpaid overtime, she was continually being overlooked or under-rewarded when it came to promotions and salary rises. She recognised that she tended not to fight this particular corner.

As a black woman in a white culture, Chloe had learned the value of self-assertion, but she now saw that she did not expect to be paid or rewarded for her dedication. She felt she had to be more than exceptional before recognition could come her way. She was doing more than others in the team but not getting her 'Brownie points'.

In relation to her foot, Chloe had the insight that she was often putting her 'best foot forward' to the point of stress, without receiving her just reward or support. Her physical foot had been showing her that something else was lacking and that an old pattern needed to be recognised and dealt with. She needed more balance between right and left, yin and yang. She needed to use her yang side to see that she was fairly treated. An underlying resentment was beginning to surface, which might affect her decisions about, and attitudes to, her work.

A few weeks later, she reported that she had requested, and been awarded, a long overdue promotion and pay award. Her right foot was much less painful and she felt that it was healing successfully at last. We had got to the root cause of the continuing tender foot.

The following exercises are based on the ideas in this chapter. Do them for yourself – it is always good for healers to check their own well-being from time to time. Having applied them to your own life, you might feel confident enough to help someone else begin to understand and explore the deeper meanings of sickness and symptoms.

Exercise
Analysing Illness

Look back to page 80 and the section entitled 'Breakdown to Breakthrough'. This looks at some of the language of life and illness and moves on to mention Judy and the exploration she made that helped her back to improve. With pen and paper to hand, use this section to help you make the following two explorations:

1. Think of a situation in your present life that you are aware is not in balance or is irking you in some way. Reflect on it as meditatively as possible. Be aware of any feelings that arise in you and of any bodily sensations that might accompany these feelings.

- Take your pen and paper and write down single, simple sentences that describe what this situation does to you when it has to be dealt with or faced. You might write phrases such as: 'It stifles me', 'It irritates me' or 'It makes me feel sick', for example.
- When you have written all you need to, reflect on the words and phrases on your paper. Highlight some of them in colour – especially any that are not only ways of expressing how you feel about the situation but may actually have converted, even if only mildly, into bodily sensations or symptoms.
- Think about any actual or attitudinal changes you might be able to make that will help you to handle the situation better next time it presents. Do you need to ask for help and support from others when perhaps you have been struggling with this situation alone?

2. Refer back to the sections beginning on page 71 about the 'conditioned well-self', 'the sick-self' and the 'true well-self'.

Think about these and try to sense how they manifest in your own life and attitudes.

- Take three separate sheets of paper or make three divisions on a larger sheet and then draw your conditioned well-self, your sick-self and your true well-self. Note the posture each takes up and the colours you choose for them. (Matchstick drawings are fine if you are not artistic.)
- Draw a 'balloon' (as in a cartoon or comic strip) coming from the mouth of each of these selves. After reflection and sensing into the nature of each, write in the balloon the words that you feel each of these aspects might want to say to you at present. Is there any action or adjustment you might need to make in your life as a result of bringing these words to awareness?

Our spiritual, mental, emotional and physical selves do not exist on separate islands. They are in constant interaction and communication, often striving to find a balance through a process of which we are usually only peripherally aware. We have to take notice of our bodies in order to achieve the mechanics of living. Thus our bodies bring to the surface those things that require our attention. These things are deeper than the physical symptoms that manifest as dis-ease.

Deep healing requires us to assist our patients in listening to the wise messages the sick-self can hold, to modify the pull of the conditioned well-self, and to make space for their true selves to blossom and flourish. The next chapter looks at the ways we can develop an awareness of the subtle bodies' colours to help us to assist patients in the search for health and vitality.

Chapter 5

Colour Healing

The chakras and colours – How chakras link to life and health –
Associating illness with the chakras – More about colours and their
qualities – Seeing, sensing and perceiving – Exercises

In considering the work of healers and of healing intervention, the idea that we work mainly with the subtle
energy field, or aura, around us is central to this book. A
basic understanding of this concept, so that we know
enough about chakras to be able to use these energy
centres as 'ways in' when healing with our hands, brings a
structured approach to healing intervention. As we saw in
Chapter 3, knowing a little more can help, both by providing a language with which to interpret healing sensations
and by firming up our inner statements of healing intent.
In this chapter, we explore the ways that increasing our
awareness of colour can help our understanding of healing
energies.

We can heal either on a sentient level and/or visually.
Many healers see colours quite naturally when healing.
Colour knowledge helps visual healing, but also means that
the non-visual healer can impart colours mentally during a

healing session, for example by *thinking* 'clear blue to the throat chakra'.

THE CHAKRAS AND COLOURS

The illustration on page 94 shows the positions and names of the chakras (see also page 34). The seven major chakras – crown, brow, throat, heart, solar plexus, sacral and root – are linked to the seven colours of the rainbow spectrum: violet for the crown, indigo for the brow, blue for the throat, green for the heart, yellow for the solar plexus, orange for the sacral and red for the root.

Each chakra is responsible for producing its spectrum colour to feed into the physical body and the auric field in order to keep the whole being healthy on every level. The alter major chakra, though important to the chakra system, is technically a minor chakra and its colours deviate from the normal rainbow chakra (see page 98).

The healthy being is a radiant, rainbow being. Part of healing intervention is to detect where this rainbow radiance may be faltering and to channel healing energy so that a subtle luminosity is restored. When our subtle energies are radiantly full of luminosity and rainbow colour, this pene-trates through to body, mind, spirit and emotions and manifests in vitality for life.

In conditions of tiredness, emotional upset or the onset of physical illness, the chakras benefit by being fed, each with its own colour. This feeding can be enabled through the hands and intent of a healer, through visualisation, with the aid of coloured lights or transparencies and with the use of crystals.

Although each chakra needs its home spectrum colour and is responsible for the production of that colour for the whole auric field, the root chakra is not only red, the solar plexus not just yellow and so on. Each and every colour may be present in each and every chakra, but if its home colour is not also strong and flowing, then unease, imbalance or disease exists within the total being. This may be transitory, since our auras, chakras and colours change many times during a day and also when we sleep.

When a healer holds their hands over the chakra energy points, the flow of healing helps to energise and balance the chakra and to restore and harmonise the colours in the chakras and in the aura. The healer does not have to be thinking colour in order for this to happen. If balance is present or being brought about in the chakra through the giving of healing, then it turns, vibrates and is full of light. It produces its own colour in a balanced shade and in correct amounts to blend with all other chakra colours, energise the auric field and produce radiant, rainbow energy for life.

Although simple direction of healing with the hands has an effect on the colours within the chakras, the healing procedure becomes more specific if the healer also visualises colour, with directed colour being used to feed and balance active or underactive chakras. Some healers quite naturally and clearly see or sense what is happening with chakras, colours and auric energies. When the chakra is sensed as lifeless, its colours and other colours in the aura may be seen or sensed as weak or pale. If the chakra is over-energised the colours may be too intense.

Healthy chakra and auric colours look like stained glass when sunlight passes through it: fairly intense, bright and translucent. When there is imbalance in us, our colours may be opaque, ethereal or faint. We may have a great deal of one colour and little of another. Because colours are also related to gifts and abilities, it is natural to have more of some than of others, but when one colour is struggling to maintain itself or is almost totally absent and another colour is too prominent, all is not well.

In the healing exercises suggested in this book, much attention is given to the chakra points. This is because at these points the state of health can be sensed, and also because if the chakras are healed, balanced and energised the self-healing mechanism can be reactivated and helped to work smoothly.

At energy interchange points, the chakras are affected by our emotions, thoughts, and reactions to and interaction with our environment. They are responsible for producing and regulating colour in our auric field. The state of our chakras affects the health of our total being, whilst the state of our total health can be read from the qualities and distribution of our chakric energies and colours.

Chakras have petals and stems, with an energy flow from petals to stems that incorporates a subtle blending and elimination system. The stems open to let unwanted energy out, and the petals open, pulse and rotate in response to life situations of all kinds. When life saddens, angers, excites or moves us, as well as when we are in different states of physical health, our chakras respond. The quality and distribution of their colours will change as they endeavour to keep us balanced and well. When things are severely out of equilibrium, the chakras may lose vitality and need special help if they are to go on doing their part in keeping us physically, mentally, emotionally and spiritually healthy.

Any colour can be present in any chakra, but the truly healthy chakra must also produce its own colour note very strongly. The distribution and quality of colours in the chakras not only gives information about our health of the moment but, when perceived or 'read' clairvoyantly, can help in knowing where our innate strengths and weaknesses lie.

How Chakras Link to Life and Health

Chakras are linked not only to colour but also to key words, developmental stages, elements, senses, to each of the seven 'bodies' in our auric field, to glands and fragrances, and to

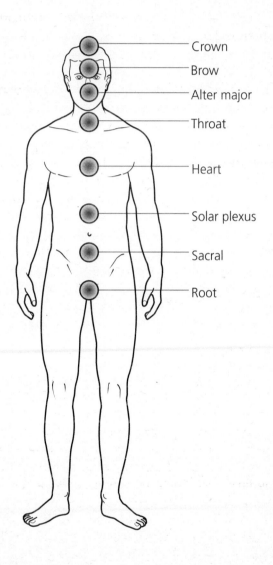

Crown

Brow

Alter major

Throat

Heart

Solar plexus

Sacral

Root

The positions and names of the most important chakras.

crystals or gemstones. (Suggestions for using crystals and fragrances for healing are given in Chapter 7.) Informing ourselves about these connections will gradually strengthen the basis of knowledge from which we can work as healers.

Root Chakra

The root chakra is located in the perineum, which is the area midway between the anus and the genitals. The petals face downwards, between the legs, and the stem faces upwards into the central column. It is naturally and healthily slightly open. The key words are rootedness, incarnation, acceptance, preservation and concept. It is linked to the developmental stage up to three/five years, and to the main colour of red and secondary colours of brown and mauve. Its element is earth. Its sense is smell. It is associated with the physical body and the gonad glands (testes in men and ovaries in women). At the root, the fragrances of cedarwood and patchouli quieten, whilst musk, lavender and hyacinth stimulate. Its crystals are smoky quartz, garnet, alexandrite, ruby, agate, bloodstone, onyx, tiger's eye and rose quartz.

Sacral Chakra

The sacral chakra is to be found approximately two fingers below the navel. The stem corresponds to the sacrum area in the spine. The key words are security, sense of others, sexuality, creativity, power, empowerment, co-creativity and sincerity. It is connected with the developmental ages from three/five to eight years. Its main colour is orange and the secondary colours are amber and gold. Its element is water, its sense taste. It is linked to the etheric body (see Chapter 6 for more information about the subtle bodies). The glandular connection is to the lymphatics. Its quietening fragrances are musk and amber, its stimulating ones are rosemary and rose geranium. Its crystals are amber, citrine, topaz, aventurine, moonstone and jasper.

Solar Plexus Chakra

The solar plexus chakra is situated just below the sternum, extending down to the navel, and the stem is in the corresponding position at the back. The key words are logic, reason, opinion, assimilation, psychic intuition and identity. Its developmental age link is from eight to twelve years. Its main colour is yellow and the secondary colours are gold and rose. The element is fire, the sense sight, and the subtle body is the astral. The glandular connection is to the adrenals. The quietening fragrances are vetivert and rose, with bergamot and ylang-ylang as stimulants. The solar plexus crystals are yellow citrine, apatite, calcite, kunzite, rose quartz, iron pyrites (fools' gold), yellow topaz and malachite.

Heart Chakra

The heart chakra is located on the same level as the physical heart but in the centre of the body, with the stem at the back. The key words and phrases are compassion, feeling, tenderness, love and search for the divine, love of others and detachment. The associated developmental age is from twelve to fifteen years, whilst its main colour is spring green with subsidiary colours of rose and rose amethyst. The element is air, the sense touch and it is connected to the subtle body known as the feeling body.

The glandular link is to the thymus. (The functioning of some glands in the body remains something of a mystery. The thymus is one of these. It is part of the lymphatic system, situated directly below the thyroid and parathyroid glands. It secretes a hormone known as thymic humoral factor. Between the ages of twelve and fifteen in the maturing human, the thymus gland begins to reduce in size. It is thought to have a connection with growth and with the progression from childhood to adulthood.) The fragrances of sandalwood and rose are quietening to the heart whilst pine and honeysuckle are stimulating. The crystals for the heart are emerald, green calcite, amber, azurite, chrysoberyl, jade, and rose and water melon tourmalines.

Throat Chakra

The throat chakra is located at the neck, with petals in front and a stem at the back. The key words are expression, responsibility, communication and universal truth. The developmental age is between fifteen and twenty-one years. The main colour is blue, the subsidiaries are silver and turquoise. The associated element is ether or akasha (see Glossary, page 192). The sense at the throat is hearing, the subtle body is the mental body, and the glandular connections are to the thyroid and parathyroids. The quietening fragrances are lavender and hyacinth. Patchouli and white musk stimulate the throat chakra. The gemstones are lapis lazuli, aquamarine, sodalite, turquoise and sapphire.

Brow Chakra

The brow chakra is located above and between the eyes, with a stem at the back of the head. The key words are spirit, completeness, inspiration, insight and command. The main colour is indigo, with subsidiaries of turquoise and mauve. The element at the brow is radium and the subtle body link is to the higher mental. The gland is the pineal. The quietening fragrances are white musk and hyacinth, and the stimulating ones are violet and rose geranium. The crystals are amethyst, purple apatite, azurite, calcite, pearl, sapphire, blue and white fluorite. (There is no associated developmental stage after the throat chakra.)

Crown Chakra

The crown chakra is situated at the top of the head, with petals facing upwards and a stem going down into the central column. The key words are soul, surrender, release and incoming will. The main colour is violet, and white and gold are the subsidiary colours. The element as given by guides is magnetum, but this has not yet been discovered for inclusion in tables of elements. The subtle body link is to the soul, ketheric or causal body, and the glandular connection is the pituitary. The quietening fragrances for the crown chakra are rosemary and bergamot, whilst violet and amber stimulate. The crystals are diamond, white tourmaline, with jade, snowy quartz and celestite.

Alter Major Chakra

The alter major chakra is located with its petals in the area of the nose. Its positive energy centre is in its stem, situated where the back of the head begins to curve round into the neck. This location corresponds to the 'old' or 'lizard' brain before the division into right and left hemispheres. The key words are instinct, resonance, rhythm, duality, devic nature and healing. The principal colour is brown and the second-ary or subsidiary colours are yellow ochre and olive green. The element is wet earth and the sense, shared with the root chakra, is smell. The subtle body link is to the instinctual and lower causal, with the same glandular connection to the adrenals as for the solar plexus. The quietening fragrances are musk and cedarwood, the stimulating ones violet and rose geranium. The crystals are carnelian, tiger's eye, snowflake obsidian, fossils and peacock stone.

ASSOCIATING ILLNESS WITH THE CHAKRAS

When looking for the deeper and symbolic meaning held by symptoms and disease, appropriate associations can be made to the chakras. Making such connections will guide us as to where the healing might most appropriately be focused. For instance, Joshua (see page 74) needed healing for his heart chakra but also for his sacral, solar plexus and root chakras. Life had closed his heart and he had been emotionally

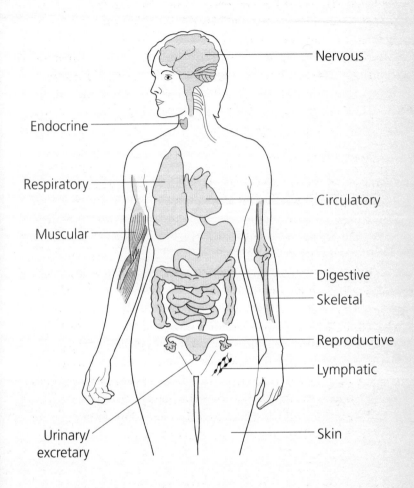

Nervous

Endocrine

Respiratory

Muscular

Circulatory

Digestive

Skeletal

Reproductive

Lymphatic

Urinary/
excretary

Skin

In a healthy person, the major systems of the body (shown simplistically above) act together in a coordinated way to ensure the smooth functioning of the body. Some, such as the muscular and skeletal systems, extend throughout the body, while the principal organs of others, like the digestive and reproductive systems, are more localised.

undernourished as a child (root chakra). His self-image and confidence in his own power was vulnerable (sacral and solar plexus). Giving healing to these chakras and teaching him to heal them himself helped his process of recovery.

My patient with aggressive breast cancer (see page 80) had always been very controlled by her conditioned well-self and had not been able to follow her heart. She needed healing for her heart chakra, but also for her sacral chakra, which is associated with power and empowerment, her solar plexus, the identity centre and fire energy chakra, and her throat chakra, to encourage her in true self-expression.

The farmer who had really always wanted to run a restaurant needed healing for his throat and sacral chakras to enable self-expression and empowerment, and also for his heart chakra because of his vulnerablility.

Judy (see page 81) needed strength in her solar plexus chakra to help her in finding her new identity, at her sacral chakra for courage to empower herself, at her throat chakra to help her self-expression, and at her alter major chakra to help her change in rhythm and pattern of life.

Chloe's (see page 84) root, sacral, heart and throat chakras needed specific healing flow. She had been loved but in many ways under-nurtured, with heavy demands put on her. This had affected her root chakra. The experience of over-rigid control by others had made her sacral chakra rather 'tight' and the general conditions of her childhood had given her a painful vulnerability that could be helped by healing her heart chakra. Never having felt that she had permission to be her true self had affected the flow and connection between her sacral and throat chakras.

Because chakra issues are complex, only a basic idea of their connections has been given here but, as a healer, simply becoming familiar with these connections will support your intuitive approach to focusing your healing sessions and will help you to understand why your intuition may draw you to certain areas. For more comprehensive information about chakras, refer to my books *Working with Your Chakras* and *Chakras – A New Approach to Healing Your Life* (see Further Reading, page 195).

MORE ABOUT COLOURS AND THEIR QUALITIES

As a non-professional healer, you will mostly use colour thoughts, intentions and visualisations as an extension to your natural, intuitive, energetic healing of the chakras, since these require no specific apparatus. I include a little more information about colours and their qualities here.

The different colours we see in our world are brought about by vibration and light. Each colour has its own specific vibration, with red being the lowest on the scale and violet the highest. (Some shades of magenta may have a higher vibration than violet, which perhaps indicates that we are moving gradually towards being able to perceive a wider range of vibrations than has previously been possible.)

There are beneficial and antagonistic aspects of colours, usually defined by shade and tone. Softer, blending or warm tones are beneficial. Harsh, garish or muddy tones are antagonistic.

On the beneficial side: *red* is for warmth, life force, energy, passion and celebration; *orange* is for vitality, initiation, creativity and sexuality; *yellow* is for light, springtime, new beginnings, clarity and joy; *green* is for growth, peace, restfulness and compassion; *blue* is for coolness, royalty, prayer, communication and healing; *indigo* and *violet* are for richness, ritual, spirituality and achievement.

On the antagonistic side: *red* is for danger, anger, wounding and desecration; *orange* is for violence, aggression, negative power and destruction; *yellow* is for criticism, cowardice, tawdriness and loss of hope; *green* is for jealousy, bitterness, misfortune and poisoning; *blue* is for coldness, cruelty, death and deterioration; *indigo* and *violet* are for aloofness, misuse of power and loss of hope.

Black is the absorption of all colours. Beneficially, it means dignity, mourning, the unknown, elegance, incubation and containment. Antagonistically, it can signify evil, nightmare, rape, death and the void. *White* is the reflection of all colours. Beneficially, it means innocence, virginity, freshness, neutrality, grace and divinity. Antagonistically, it is blankness, harshness, shallowness and cowardly surrender.

Silver and *gold* are the colours of the sun and moon. Traditionally, silver represents the feminine principle and gold the masculine. On the beneficial side, *silver* stands for cleansing, gentle strength, purity, natural rhythms, ebb and flow, mirroring, reflections and vision. In its antagonistic aspect, it is coldness, harshness, rigidity and treachery. Beneficially, *gold* is abundance, the divine, high spiritual attainment, warmth, harmony and perfection. Antagonistically, it represents materialism, opulence, false values and false images.

Pink in beneficial shades means love, tenderness, romance, birth, childlikeness and fragrance. Antagonistically, it stands for faint-heartedness, childishness, lack of taste and artificiality.

Brown has the beneficial attributes of fertility, containment, seed-time, harvest and mellowness. Antagonistically, it represents blockage, filth, obstacles, depression and despair.

Sometimes the difference between the beneficial and antagonistic side of a colour is experienced in the shade or tone as suggested above. At other times the context in which the colour is experienced will define whether its nature is beneficial or antagonistic. All meanings should be seen not as portents but as messages that help to bring clarity and choice.

Developing Awareness of Auric Colour

As a healer, being able to see the colours and shades of a patient's aura is a great help in knowing what a patient

needs and perhaps in making a deeper level, symbolic diagnosis of what is not well. Some healers sense the colours and
the quality each shade or tone is carrying, without actually
'seeing'. Others say they can 'smell' colour and whether it is
in positive or negative manifestation. It is possible gradually
to come to know a colour, tone or shade by its energy – or
simply an inner knowing (see Sensing the Energy of
Colours, page 105).

People who feel themselves drawn to healing and motiv-
ated to practise it often find that their sensitivities develop,
and an increasing amount of subtle information floods in.
You can struggle to develop colour awareness or vision, but
mostly it just happens with practice. You suddenly realise
that you simply know such things as: this patient needs more
yellow or more blue; this root chakra is not vibrating as well
as it might because it needs feeding with a soft red; that
patient is manifesting such a bright shade of orange in their
spectrum that other colours are overwhelmed and the whole
system is out of balance. Having a basic knowledge of and
vocabulary about colours and chakras helps you to express
what you are sensing or perceiving when you heal, so that
more specific healing interventions emerge naturally.

If you want to be more aware of colour in your healing
and use colours more consciously and fluently in your
healing intent, simply inform yourself about them and then
relax until the day comes when you realise that they have
become a natural part of your healing thinking and perception. You may or may not be actively seeing the colours
by then, but you will be perceiving them through your
senses and sensitivity.

SEEING, SENSING AND PERCEIVING

When dealing with subtle energies, colours and the auric
field, the whole question of sensing, seeing and perception

needs to be considered. I have found that many healers in training hold themselves back or create an obstacle in the development of their sensitivity by holding an expectation that the perception of subtle energies has to be an actual seeing with the physical eyes. This is not so and, I believe, is the actuality for only a very limited number of individuals. Perception is much broader and more complex than physical seeing.

In the outer world, as sighted individuals we take seeing our environment for granted and may have minimal awareness of the other complex ways in which information about the environment is gathered by us. Any blind person can tell us that a sightless world is still a perceptual world. When physical sight is denied, data floods in through other senses, which become more sharpened.

The first exercise in this book (see page 18) was designed to help you become more aware of the auric or energy field that surrounds each one of us. We extend, energetically, beyond our physical bodies. This subtle energy field can be subtly perceived or electrically sensed but of itself has sensate perception. We take in information through sight, hearing, touching, smelling and tasting, but something other is added in our full perception which is more than knowledge and experience and is a part of the renowned 'sixth sense'. Not only is this something other added when all our other senses are functioning, but it also exists when the other senses are, for some reason, disabled, blocked or muted.

If we sit quietly in a dark room, we can often sense whether it is empty or furnished. This can happen even without the clue of noise, which would tell us something by the way it echoed or was absorbed. We can sense if there is furniture or other objects, because gradually the space taken, even by inanimate objects, imposes itself upon our energy field and our subtle perception.

We would also sense if other people were present, but it is

easier then to say that we heard breathing, or were aided by our sense of smell. The fact remains that even our natural, moment-by-moment perception of our world is more complex than we might think. We are always employing something other, something extra, in our 'reading' of what is around us, and this affects our action and interaction within the environment at any given time.

Part of what urges you to be a healer will probably be a natural, strong access to this 'something other'. Training this extra factor in perception will lead you to sense, know, perceive and perhaps (but only perhaps) hear and see other worlds as clearly and with the same organs of perception as those you employ in the outer, everyday world.

Knowing that energetic perception is aided by a factor in addition to the usual interaction of our five senses will help you to become subtly but accurately aware when you are healing, and to interpret this awareness to inform your healing sessions. The more open you stay to perception at the subtle levels being complex yet delicate, the more you will develop expertise in interpreting feeling and sensing. This sensing is precise and is often described as a 'seeing' and 'hearing' or even as a 'touching', a 'smelling' or a 'tasting', although the physical senses are not directly involved.

Exercise
Sensing the Energy of Colours

Working with a friend or partner is always helpful when practising healing development exercises of all kinds. It helps if you can prepare notes and help each other with the practicalities of the procedure, but it is also possible to work alone with a growth of sensitivity exercise such as this one. The ideal would be to share it with an interested partner or friend to begin with and then to use it alone from time to time to train and sharpen your perceptions.

- Prepare some sheets of paper on which you have vividly painted or crayoned the colours of the rainbow. (Use one sheet per colour. A4 or an A4 sheet squared is about the right size.) It may not be easy to find an indigo paint or crayon, but try to have the basics of red, orange, yellow, green, blue and violet. The violet should be a deep, rich colour, not pale lavender or mauve.

- Preparing the sheets is part of the exercise. Take time and care with each one and, as you colour them, allow yourself to feel the energy of the colour. Maybe a particular colour will have particular memories associated with it for you. Let these memories flow, and sense the energy and atmosphere that goes with them, unless any are particularly difficult or unhappy. (On the whole, if you have good, clear, positive colours, difficult memories will not be aroused by this exercise but if this does happen leave that colour aside until you have talked the memories through with a friend, partner, another healer or a counsellor. Transpersonal or psychosynthesis counsellors would be particularly open to discussing issues that may arise from such an exercise as this; see Glossary, page 192.)

- Sense how each colour affects you and where in your body you tend to respond to it. You may feel tensions in muscles or organs, or you may experience mood changes that are linked for you to the stimuli of certain colours. Familiarise yourself with the energy that comes from the different colours and focus on the response and slight mood changes you feel in your own energy field.

- After a while, get your partner to arrange the colours in random order whilst you turn away, or close your eyes. If you are working alone, shuffle the colours around on the floor or table, whilst your eyes are closed.

- Still with your eyes closed, get your partner to select one colour at a time (or do so yourself) and hold it up to you, bringing it either close to your outstretched hands and/or into your energy field around the level of either your solar plexus or your brow chakra until the coloured sheet is about 15 centimetres (6 inches) away from you. See if you can sense the colour on the paper without opening your eyes. Test out whether you sense it better with your hands or when it is near your solar plexus or your brow chakra. You might find that you sense it first with your hands and also feel an answering response in either your solar plexus or your brow chakra or perhaps both/all of these.

• When you have done some initial work with sensing the colours one after the other, you may decide that you want to focus on a particular colour in everyday life for a period of several days. One week you might choose violet, another orange, another green and so on, until you feel very familiar with the basic spectrum colours and their energies.

If this exercise works well for you with the clear, true colours of the spectrum, you can progress to more subtle shades and colours such as pinks, mauves, ambers, different shades of green and blue, and experiment with the more neutral colour range of brown, grey, mauve, black and white.

Exercises
Meditations Using Colour

Once you feel that you are becoming more sensitive to the energy of colour in the outer world, it is a good idea to explore and use colour in your inner world – seeing it in visual meditation with your inner eye, in your inner land-scape. Here are two colour visualisations or meditations that you can practise. The first also helps you to be more aware of the chakras and their areas of influence.

1. Meadow Meditation

- Making sure that you will be undisturbed, sit or lie in a comfortable but symmetrically balanced position. Wrap yourself in a blanket for comfort and warmth if you wish, remembering that in meditation your body may lose heat. Unless you are sitting cross-legged or in a lotus position, do not cross your legs at the ankles or knees. Do not fold or cross your arms. Have the palms of your hands open and curved, and facing upwards. You can balance your hands, palm open and up, on your knees if you are sitting and on the floor beside you if you are lying down.
- Be aware of the rhythm of your breathing – do not force your breath or try to calm it. Simply allow it to find its own natural rhythm. Gradually bring that rhythm into your heart centre or chakra, and sense how each in-breath and out-breath feeds, relaxes and opens your heart chakra.
- Become aware of the column of subtle energy that runs through the centre of your body. With your breath, follow this from just above the crown of your head down through the centre of your body, out through your root chakra and into the earth. Breathe with this direction of the energy flow for five or six breath sequences (in/out = one breath sequence), breathing in at the point just above your crown chakra and out into the earth, returning to the point above your crown chakra to take the next in-breath.
- Finish this part of the meditation on an exhalation into the earth. Then, visualising a deep but soft, rosy red coming up from the earth on your next in-breath, breathe up as far as your root chakra and flood this chakra with the warming, energising colour and breathe out again into the earth. As you breathe red up from the earth and into your root chakra for the third or fourth

time, find yourself in a meadow in your inner landscape.

- The meadow is flooded with the wondrous shades of light and warmth that come from a rosy sunrise. The day is beginning and you are awake and alive to witness it. See the colours and the objects in your meadow, hear the sounds, smell the fragrances, touch the textures and taste the tastes. Breathe naturally and normally. Rejoice in the gifts of earth and life as the rosy sunrise unfolds around you.

- From the meadow there is a clear path that leads along level ground and then beside a river with a bridge over it. Further on you can see that the path begins to climb, leading to hills and slopes beyond. As you follow the path to the bridge, the light around you becomes orangey, as the full morning sun prepares to break through.

- Breathing in this orange light, you come to the bridge over the river and as you stand on the bridge it seems that the whole world is bathed in orange. It reflects from the sky and from the water and bathes you. You can feel the power of the river beneath you. It is fast-flowing and vital, and in the movement of the water every shade of orange and amber is visible, alive and at play. Trees grow on the riverbanks and for the moment they, too, seem to be orange. Even the birds in the branches and the rabbits at play on the riverbanks have an orangey glow about them, and the air is full of vigour and life force.

- From the bridge, the path begins to climb, sloping easily upwards. Ahead of you, fascinatingly, you can see a place where the morning sun is shining directly on to some seemingly randomly planted sunflowers. You follow the path to this spot, where you step aside for a few moments to savour the fragrance, colour and beauty of the sunflowers as they open themselves up and stretch to the sunlight. The morning yellow of the sun bathes you too, and for a few moments you live in a sunshiny yellow world, feeling yourself fed with the promise of midday warmth that the morning sun is already bringing.

- From this slightly raised point in your landscape you can see the path ahead and the path you have taken. No one else is about. There is only you, the light, the plants, animals and the river. You feel fed with a sense of ownership and by the light of the sun that has become yellow, flooding over and into you. Digest all this for a few moments and then, as you decide to step back to the path and move on, let your hand brush over the face of a sunflower and notice how it becomes yellowed by the pollen dust, symbol of fecundity.

- The path goes on, climbing gently, and as it does so you get more and more of an overview of your landscape. The vegetation around you is lush and green as you enter a wooded area. The sun is shining through the leaves on the trees and, as you look up, the delicate, spring-like green of the light-filled leaves seems to become a part of you. You are in a green, leafy glade full of green light as the leaves filter the brightness of the sun on this beautiful day. Birds are singing and you feel your heart opening. You touch trees and plants and feel at one with them. The birdsong has a particularly melodious quality and as you bathe in green light it seems that your heart sings too.

- Although the path has apparently only sloped easily and gently beneath your feet, as you come out of the wooded area you notice with surprise that you have come beyond the tree line on to rocky and slatey ground, with only intermittent sparse plants with shallow, parched roots. On this magical morning, however, the blue slate, bathed in sun, gives out a bright, clear colour that glows like the blue of lapis lazuli.

- As you bathe in this colour your throat chakra awakens and, as the world is your own, you sing and sound some clear notes, enjoying the echo of them that comes back to you and reverberates around. You can see over your landscape, back to the meadow where this path began, and on beyond the hills and slopes to the sea, which also glows blue and sparkles in the sunlight. The air is clear and the sounds you make are clear too. The blue light is cooling, cleansing and invigorating at one and the same time.

- Now the path leads around to the more shady side of the slopes. Although you are at a vantage point in your landscape, the path is wide, safe and undemanding. The shady side of the slopes, still with the blue slate covering them, has a glow of its own and you realise that you are being bathed in indigo light.

- You allow this colour of mystery to feed into your being and as you do so you become particularly aware of the path you have walked today. You see where you have come from and then you see where the path leads – all the possibilities it has to offer and that you could choose to take. You feel an ethereal glow, a leap of spirit, a sense of joy and potential, a renewed perception of meaning in life.

- From this point the path leads on quite steeply. This last piece of your morning journey takes a little more exertion, but ahead of you there is a real vantage point where you know you will feel lord or lady of all you survey. This point above you is bathed in a bright, deep violet light of its own. You long to bathe in it, and so the steepness of the path becomes easier.

- When you arrive at the highpoint there is a seat to rest on, right in the centre of the violet light. As you sit there, you feel warmed by the sun but cleansed and invigorated by the violet light. You get a sense of communion with your higher self here and a renewed sense of purpose and meaning in your life. You feel energised and at peace.

- After a few minutes, you open your eyes to find that the intense violet light has faded and you are sitting in a sunny spot with a commanding view over your landscape and a clear stream trickling near by. You refresh yourself from the clear water and know that you can either begin your journey back to the meadow where you began and descend to it gradually or that, if you just think yourself into the meadow, you will be there instantly.
- Whichever way you choose, take yourself back, now, to the meadow and from there to your awareness of your breath in your heart centre and then to your body sitting or lying in your everyday surroundings. Let the petals of your heart chakra fold in, like those of a rose, gently but not tightly, protecting the centre but allowing the fragrance of the rose to interact with the environment. Rest a while and then resume your normal, everyday activities.

2. Rainbow Meditation

- Making sure that you will be undisturbed, sit or lie in a comfortable but symmetrically balanced position. Wrap yourself in a blanket for comfort and warmth if you wish, remembering that in meditation your body may lose heat. Unless you are sitting cross-legged or in a lotus position, do not cross your legs at the ankles or knees. Do not fold or cross your arms. Have the palms of your hands open and curved, and facing upwards. You can balance your hands, palm open and up, on your knees if you are sitting and on the floor beside you if you are lying.
- Be aware of the rhythm of your breathing – do not force your breath or try to calm it. Simply allow it to find its own natural rhythm. Gradually bring that rhythm into your heart centre or chakra and sense how each in-breath and out-breath feeds, relaxes and opens your heart chakra.

- Become aware of the column of subtle energy that runs through the centre of your body. With your breath, follow this from just above the crown of your head down through the centre of your body, out through your root chakra and into the earth. Breathe with this direction of the energy flow for five or six breath sequences (in/out = one breath sequence), breathing in at the point just above your crown chakra and out into the earth, returning to the point above your crown chakra to take the next in-breath.
- Finish this part of the meditation on an exhalation into the earth. As you breathe up again, focus on your heart chakra before finding yourself in a meadow in your inner landscape. Take the opportunity to activate your inner senses, see the colours and the objects around you, hear the sounds, smell the fragrances, touch the textures and taste the tastes. Breathe naturally and normally. From your meadow you can see your inner landscape opening out and, as you look, you see that there is a rainbow, bright, translucent and sparkling. You also see that there is a point not too far away from you where it seems that you can, in this inner world of yours, enter the place where the rainbow colours join the earth.
- Go to this place and find that you can indeed stand at the centre of the rainbow, bathed in all its colours. Feel the quality of translucent light drenched with colour. Accept the rainbow colours into your own body, feel them healing you and sense your response to them. The whole spectrum is here: red, orange, yellow, green, blue, indigo and violet.
- When you have had enough of this magical, energising and healing experience, step out of the rainbow, return to the place where you entered your meadow and from here to your awareness of your body and the rhythm of your breath in your heart chakra. Let the petals of your heart chakra close in gently, protecting your heart

energy without tightly sealing this centre. When you feel grounded and centred again, return to your normal, everyday activities.

Exercise
Mentally Sending and Receiving Colours

This exercise works best with a partner or maybe a small group of interested people. If this is totally impossible, some suggestions for using it by yourself are also given.

- Sit opposite your partner, or facing a small group. Each of you should begin by becoming aware of your breathing, letting the rhythm find its own level and then using the breath at your heart chakra level to activate your heart energy. This creates the atmosphere in which to work.
- One person then tries to visualise one of six of the spectrum colours clearly and strongly, projecting the visualisation out into the room or towards the partner or group. The colours are: red, orange, yellow, green, blue and violet.
- The partner or group try to sense the energy of the colour and where in the body it is received or what area of the body it activates. Receiving the energy and feeling it in the body is initially more important than being accurate about which colour is being transmitted but, if you practise together, an accuracy in sensing the colour itself will gradually grow.
- Although people vary in where they might be activated in the body by a certain colour, it is most usual to receive red in the root or heart chakra areas, orange at sacral or throat, yellow at solar plexus, brow or crown, green at heart or root, blue at throat or sacral and violet at crown, brow or solar plexus. The chakras may feel activated or

organs in the area of the chakras may respond to the colours. Energisation may be felt at the front and/or the back of the body.

- If you have a small group working together, a variation on this exercise is to have one person sitting in the centre of the group with the whole group visualising the colour. Your colour sheets are useful here: the group waits until the central person has their eyes shut; then a colour sheet can be held up to the group as a silent signal about which colour to focus on. After three or four minutes, senders and receivers can comment on the atmosphere and reactions produced by the focus on each particular colour.

- If you can only work alone, you can use the technique of invocation to activate this exercise for yourself. Although you will know what colour you are invoking, you can still sense its energies and qualities, receive it in your body and perceive the atmosphere it brings into your environment.

- Work with one colour at a time, maybe one each day or every other day. Read the section on invocation on page 52. Decide which colour you want to work with, do the heart centre breathing recommended above, close your eyes and say something simple such as: 'I invoke the colour orange in a pure, healing and energising form' and then spend a few moments bathing in the colour and noting your reactions to it.

Exercise
Colour Healing Sequence

This healing sequence is an expansion of the earlier healing sequences (see pages 39 and 42), adding colour to what has gone before. Practise first with a partner if possible.

- Choose whether you want to work with your patient sitting (see page 39) or lying down (see page 42). Carefully re-read the instructions for the healing sequence you have chosen. Pay particular attention to your preparation with running energy and making a healing invocation.
- Information about the alter major chakra is given on page 98 and you may like to include this in your healing sequence now. Remember that it has its positive electrical energy point at the back of the head and its negative one at the front in the region of the nose. Therefore at this chakra you need to remember to put your left hand at the front and your right hand at the back. It is usually best if you go to the alter major after you have dealt with the crown, then if you want to stand on the other side of your patient, it is easy to do so without needing to change position more than once.
- As you go through the chakra points and heal the areas of the body requiring special attention, interpret the energies you pick up from your patient as colour. Think of each colour as you are working and gradually have the courage to visualise colour flowing through your hands into the chakras.

  As you gain in experience and sensitivity, you will instinctively know which auric colours need balancing or feeding, and whether a particular colour is almost nonexistent, but to begin with you cannot go wrong if, as you heal each chakra point, you visualise the principal colour for that chakra clearly and translucently, seeing it as stained glass appears when sunlight passes through it. (The colours are rosy red for the root, orange for the sacral, yellow for the solar plexus, green for the heart, blue for the throat, indigo for the brow, violet for the crown and a rich, clear, translucent, reddish brown for the alter major if you have decided to include it.)
- For bodily areas requiring special attention, soft reds are

warming, pink is comforting, orange and amber are energising, yellow awakens and lightens, green soothes and encourages flow where there may be blockage, blue cools and quietens pain, and indigo and violet aid relaxation and calm any fear or panic.
- When you have finished the healing session carry out the energetic separation and rounding off as for all healing sequences.

As you practise this exercise and other healing sequences, you will begin to realise that sometimes your hands are picking up information from your patient's energy field and chakras, and sometimes they are aiding the healing flow to come through you to the patient. There is quite a difference in energy between sensing your patients' energy fields and actually channelling healing. When you feel sensations in the palms of your hands like prickling, heat or coolness, you are usually reading what is going on in your patient's energy field, or aura. When you feel a flow through your hands and fingers or that you are drawn intuitively to certain body areas, this is the healing flow using you as its channel and for its direction.

As you go on to use more and more specific healing procedures, it is important to endeavour to make this differentiation, so that you can be more involved in reading or sensing what is required and deciding which healing exercises to use to augment the healing session.

Chakras and colours are important in our energy fields. Learning to sense colour helps you to develop your subtle perceptions as a healer. The energy field is also made up of layers, related to and interacting with the chakras and each also having its own colour and electrical energy. These layers are often referred to as subtle bodies. The next chapter describes them and their functions.

Chapter 6

The Auric Layers

Robert's story – Subtle energy system – The etheric body –
The astral body – The feeling body – The mental body –
The higher mental body – The soul, ketheric or causal body –
Wholeness of being – Exercises

ROBERT'S STORY

Robert was a keen amateur tennis player. He had been attracted to learning more about healing ever since a friend with healing gifts treated a strained leg tendon for him. It healed quickly and strongly, in time for Robert to take part in a tournament to which he had been particularly looking forward. He felt there was no real reason why he should assume that he too might be able to heal as a result of his experience, but the idea persisted. He decided to come to some of my healing practise sessions for developing healers.

When Robert received healing from others in the group he felt very moved and was aware of something happening within and around him. When he gave healing to others, they felt a strong sense of healing surrounding them.

Despite these reports and encouragement, and although he never missed a group session and assiduously practised everything I could teach, for a long time Robert said that he experienced nothing at all when he was endeavouring to be a healing channel. He had to rely on the encouraging reports from others.

When Robert had been introduced to the first stage of sensing the subtle energy field (see page 18), at his first session with the group, he had been fascinated and excited. When healing, he could always sense the edge of his patient's energy field but he wanted more, and felt disappointed with his own perceptions of his development.

When we worked with training colour perception Robert began to sense the different colour vibrations and energies, and felt more secure about accurately locating each chakra. He insisted that much of this was common sense or very transient. Obviously his deprecation of his own gifts and of anything he might briefly sense did not help him in his desire to develop and train his subtle sensitivities. To want or expect too much too soon can be an obstacle to laying the basic foundations on which to build.

It was working with and discussing subtle anatomy and the broader subtle energies of the aura that caused things ultimately to fall into place for Robert. He felt perfectly at home with the idea of different layers and planes, and related strongly to the notion of sensing subtle textures. As a veil lifted for him, he was at last able to value the very multi-faceted nature of perception. I felt that Robert had finally opened that layer of his heart chakra that enables entry to the contemplative state in which all subtle perceptions are at their strongest. When this happens – and it is worth persevering until it does – subtle experience becomes more vivid and meaningful and expands effortlessly. (The exercise on page 128 supports and assists this process.)

I have included Robert's story here because he is typical of many for whom the opening of subtle perception happens very gradually, with a lot of doubts along the way. Although the ultimate aim must always be to return to simplicity, the more areas you learn about and explore, even very tentatively, the more opportunities there are for your perception of subtle energies to develop and for you to find the key that enables a growth of confidence.

SUBTLE ENERGY SYSTEM

As I have already outlined (see page 91), the chakras are wheels and centres of light, colour and energy. They interpenetrate with the physical body, and affect and are affected by our physical, mental, emotional and spiritual states. They carry links to the body's glandular system and are, in a sense, refined glands.

There are myriad subtle energy pathways interpenetrating with our physical bodies. They are called meridians and nadis (see also page 32) and are like refined arteries and veins. The nadis run everywhere, like numberless branching and intersecting minor roads or pathways over a territory. The meridians are more major pathways finely connecting the major organs to each other and carrying energy from the major organs throughout the whole of our complex physical and interconnecting subtle systems.

The eight major chakras occur where there is major production or crossing of nadis and meridians. Numerous other minor chakras form where there is a less busy production and fewer crossing points. Most of these minor chakras are connected to organs of the body such as the spleen, the liver, kidneys and pancreas.

The eyes, ears, hands, feet and bony structure of the head carry links to all the major and minor chakras in the body and are used as focus points for the imparting of finely tuned healing in disciplines such as iridology, metamorphic technique, reflexology and cranial osteopathy.

THE ETHERIC BODY

In esoteric teaching, there are seven layers to our total being
and energy field, including the physical body. Each organ of
the body has a subtle counterpart, and the sum total of
meridians, nadis, chakras and subtle organ counterparts
forms the 'body' or auric layer closest to the physical. This is
known as the etheric body or layer. (Names for the different

Soul, ketheric or causal body
Higher mental body
Lower mental body
Feeling body
Astral body
Etheric body
Physical body

The physical body and the six layers of the auric field.

layers, bodies or planes vary throughout esoteric teaching.
Here I use the terms I have been taught by my guide.) It is
a subtle 'double' of the physical layer and the densest of the
subtle bodies. In disease, the etheric body has to repair itself
before the physical organs and function can return to
normal. Most healing for the physical body is received first
at the etheric level. When this is balanced and invigorated,
the healing permeates through to the physical level, or layer.

When any part of the physical body is amputated or removed, its etheric essence remains. The phantom limb is a medically accepted fact. The etheric body may be very traumatised and need intensive healing but it remains whole. Losing a physical organ does not mean losing its etheric counterpart. This is one of the reasons why the physical body is able to adapt and carry on functioning even when a relatively important organ has been removed.

With the modern drugs of allopathic medicine, we live under a delusion that healing can happen quite quickly. Certainly many unpleasant symptoms can be eased but when symptoms disappear the journey of healing is not necessarily complete, especially for the etheric body. Recovery from illness needs time, rest and tender loving care, whether the presenting symptoms have been miraculously 'cured' or suppressed or not.

There is no denying that allopathy has produced many breakthroughs in healing, but the subtle bodies have their own healing rhythm and may be adversely affected by the strong medications that remove physical symptoms. Resting when ill is sometimes seen as weak or undignified, but our present way of life can be too demanding for our intricate constitutions, and society often requires that we push ourselves too far. As healers bent on understanding the whole spectrum of healing, we need to help our patients to honour the healing process by taking the time to heal that is required by the etheric body.

When the etheric body is 'sensed', it feels tingly, prickly and 'electric'. Its colour is orangey. This layer has strong links to the sacral chakra and the lymphatic glands. The plane of being to which the etheric body helps us to connect is known as the etheric plane. It is full of echoes of the experiences we have on the physical plane. When working as a healer or to develop your spiritual perception, it can be important to be aware of keeping the etheric body, and the immediately surrounding etheric plane, bright and active. It can become rather heavy and, instead of being a bright, energised web around us, become more like a dust-filled cobweb. The exercise on page 134 describes how to keep personal links to the etheric body and plane working at their optimum level for you.

THE ASTRAL BODY

Moving out from the physical body, the second subtle layer or body, known as the astral body, consists of subtle flowing energies. Its colour is yellow gold, rose or a clear, slightly electric, silvery blue. It has strong links to the solar plexus chakra and the adrenal glands. When sensed, it feels cool and fluid. The plane of being to which it helps us connect is known as the astral plane.

A frequently reported aspect of near-death experience is of being in another part of the room, usually high up near the ceiling, watching what is happening to the physical body. Those who have survived serious accidents have reported watching their physical body being rescued or treated, while their consciousness or essence waits at a distance, away from the physical pain and distress. In these experiences the awareness is withdrawn to the astral body or plane.

Many people become attracted to the spiritual path because of the possibility of learning astral travel. In this altered state of consciousness, journeys through time and space, and even bi-location, become possible. Anyone who wants to work specifically with esoteric development of the astral body should consult a well-established esoteric school or find a trusted teacher.

The higher astral plane, as described by esotericists and sensitives, is very beautiful. It has flowing landscapes and healing temples. It is the plane where there is a loving contact with guides, helpers and angelic beings and the one where we are met and welcomed when, in death, we finally leave our physical bodies.

Lower layers of the astral plane are less attractive. Thought forms and negative entities populate these regions. Some of the experiences of bad drug trips and schizophrenia can come from a vulnerability that precipitates an unwanted breakthrough into these realms. These vulnerable states usually mean that the chakra stems have become too open, with the natural flow from petals to stem being upset.

The chakra stems open intermittently to eliminate subtle toxins, but when they become too open they may not seal themselves properly or control this natural flow. An open stem can attract an unwanted infiltration of energies from the lower astral plane and result in mental confusion, frightening and vivid visions, and irrational promptings. Damaged stems need subtle healing energy, as from a healer, to help their repair. Some healers and psychic workers choose to specialise in working with people who have become disorientated by these influences.

THE FEELING BODY

The third subtle layer, moving outwards from the physical body, is termed the feeling body. It has strong links to the heart chakra and the thymus gland (linked to growth and maturation). The feeling body is a very pale, light green in colour. When sensed it feels warmer, softer and less fluid than the astral body but it is also very full of vitality.

When awareness is projected into the feeling body, perceptions are considerably sharpened and heightened. People and objects may be experienced in a special way. Tapping into the feeling body layer enables us to enter a state known as contemplation, which is a deep level of meditation (see page 128). In this state there is full identification with other people, trees, rocks, plants, crystals or animals.

We experience from within and sense the nature of other beings and life forms, sharing, as much as it is ever possible to share, the nature of other humans or life forms and their rhythms and life cycles.

It is the feeling body that enables the ultimate, mystical experience of total oneness or unity with the universe, described by contemplatives, mystics and poets. Those earth-shattering, totally satisfying moments of unity with a lover where you lose yourselves in each other are also one of the products of connection with the feeling body.

Using more heart colours in your decor, clothing or environment helps to awaken and open your access to your feeling body. Robert's (see page 118) breakthrough in subtle sensing and perception came when dogged persistence with his healing development strengthened his link to his feeling body.

THE MENTAL BODY

The fourth level out from the physical body is the mental body. When sensed, it has a fluid but tingly texture. It is reflective, and glows with very subtle shades of blue, silver and turquoise. These are the colours of the throat chakra, to which it has a strong link. The glandular connection is to the thyroid.

As its name implies, the mental body is partly connected to intellect and abstract thought, to the world of ideas, conceptual blueprints and archetypes. It links us to those unseen patterns, subtle nuances and barely heard sounds which are aspects of complex communication. It enables us to apprehend, name and implement certain volatile and abstract aspects of the universe, and make use of them in life and incarnation. This includes our integral awareness of, and struggle with, divine principles or qualities. We feel a true sense of human potential when our societies reflect qualities such as peace, love, justice, respect and right relationship to power. We struggle to define these in life. Being in touch with our mental bodies and the mental plane helps us to find integrity.

Healing for the throat chakra and mental body helps concepts to change so that if a patient is frightened or convinced that an illness, condition or lifestyle resulting from chronic disease or impairment cannot be improved in any way, a new, more positive attitude can emerge and greater symbolic understanding is enabled.

THE HIGHER MENTAL BODY

This is the fifth layer working outwards from the physical body. It is linked to the brow chakra and to the pineal gland. The higher mental body is of a supremely light and subtle substance. It reflects deep indigo and amethyst colours and when sensed is filmy, sheer, ethereal, pulsating and cool.

The higher mental body is the 'garment' we wear for our highest levels of meditational experience, communication with other planes and intense moments of inspiration.

The mental plane is filled with sheer and pulsating waves. The inspiration that gives birth to ideas originates here, before it becomes clothed with language or form. It is the plane of divine principle, pure archetypal impulses and of the archangelic beings: Michael, Uriel, Raphael and Gabriel. (See Glossary, page 192, for more detail on pure archetypal impulses and angels.)

THE SOUL, KETHERIC OR CAUSAL BODY

These are alternative names for the sixth and final subtle body, encountered when moving through the auric field, outwards from the physical. It is linked to the crown chakra and the pituitary gland. It glows with intense but pale and fine violet light. When sensed, it feels flowing and silky. It has a warm, soft glow.

The ketheric body is an evolutionary imprint or reflection from the soul. In incarnation this layer can affect us through those subtle memories from other lives that cause us to react to positive or negative stimuli in a manner not directly explicable in terms of our present life experience. Unexpectedly intense or so-called irrational fears, 'free floating' anxieties, *déjà vu* experiences and exceptional giftedness are all examples of the interpenetration of the soul, ketheric or causal body.

This layer of the auric field holds the imprint of the learning intentions we have made for this lifetime. Connection with this body and plane will help us to see a higher pattern, purpose and direction in our lives.

WHOLENESS OF BEING

Working with the wider energy field surrounding each one of us begins (as in Sensing the Energy Field, page 18) with an overall electrical sensing. It progresses through an awareness of chakras as energy and colour points, interpenetrating with our physical bodies, to an ever clearer impression of the distinct layers within our aura of being.

The more we feel into and accept the multi-faceted and rainbow nature of our wider substance, the more we realise the many complexities that can affect our health and wellbeing. We are finely balanced. Channelled healing energy is equally finely attuned and infiltrates all our layers, energy points, subtle bodies and layers. Maximising our potential makes our response to life and incarnation total and healthful. Glimpsing the wonder of our wider fineness of being also helps us, as healers, to appreciate the refined nature of our extended potential for perception.

Channelled healing automatically seeks out and balances the different subtle levels, but as your healing expertise develops, you may want to carry out more conscious and specific healing techniques. Giving extra attention to the etheric body, for instance, strengthens the potential for healing to manifest at the physical level and for depleted organs to be energised. Specific healing for the astral body may help people who grieve, fear death, are mentally ill or suffer with bad dreams or nightmares.

Consciously treating the feeling body will help people who want to be more perceptive and open to wider aspects of being. It will also help those who are too open to unseen influences and who tend to 'take the weight of the world' on their shoulders.

Healing the mental body will help people who fear to speak their own truth or who are out of touch with the real value of their own integrity. For those who live in too abstract a world, it will help with the ability to know what they are feeling, whilst they are feeling it.

Working with the higher mental body will help people to connect with the energy of the true spirit of their being and to find wider meaning in life. Healing for the soul, ketheric or causal body helps those who feel directionless to find life's purpose once more and to feel connected to something higher, but personal. It can help those who are going through personal tragedy to feel less abandoned and to find a perspective for what has happened.

Exercise
Enabling the Contemplative Level of Perception

This exercise is good for helping the development of a healer's sensitivity and ability to 'read' the patient.

You need a plant, a crystal, and connection with a tree, an animal or another person. It takes practice to establish this

level of the heart chakra as one that will open for you whenever you want to attune to different levels of awareness and
perception. You are recommended to repeat the exercise at
least once a week but not more than every other day over a
period of time. Whichever option you have chosen from
plant, crystal, tree, animal or other person, work with that
first choice two or three times, so that you can get a sense of
progression. It is then important to vary your experience by
moving on to another available option and staying with that
for two or three times. Keep up a variety, but after trying
new options always return to former ones.

Before you begin the process below, make your selection.
If you are going to use a plant or crystal, have it near you. If
you are choosing to attune to a small domestic animal, you
can take it on your knee or simply make sure it is in the same
room. If you are attuning to another person, sit opposite
them, if possible, attuning to each other at the same time. If
you are attuning to an outdoor animal or a tree, you will
need to be able to sit or, perhaps in summer, lie down in its
vicinity. Always try to touch the animal or tree before you
begin this attunement.

During the exercise the plant, crystal, animal, tree or
person you have chosen to work with is referred to as an
'ally'. The practice leads you to a point where you endeavour
to let your energy field blend with the ally and let the energy
field of the ally flow into you. It is important to make sure
that your chosen ally is one you feel comfortable with.

The flowing of one energy into the other is a state of
contemplation and it is important, as you first practise this
exercise, only to allow the contemplative state to last for two
or three minutes. If you know that there is a time limit at this
stage, part of you will honour it and you will move back into
a lighter state of meditation after the allowed time without
the need to use a timer. If you feel uncertain of this, you can
prerecord the instructions for this practice, leaving a two- or
three-minute gap on your tape before you speak the next

words. As you grow used to the sensation, you can expand
the time up to ten or fifteen minutes.

Remember that contemplation is a deep meditative state
and allow plenty of time for the transition from contemplation, through ordinary level meditation, to everyday life.

- Making sure that you will be undisturbed, sit or lie
  comfortably with your body in a symmetrical position
  and your back well supported if necessary. Sit in a cross-
  legged or lotus posture (see page 187), if you wish, but
  otherwise do not cross your legs at your ankles or knees.
  Have your arms and hands by your side, with your
  palms curved open and facing upwards if lying down, or
  hands balanced on your knees, palms curved open and
  facing upwards, if sitting. Pay particular attention to the
  balance and alignment of your head and neck as this
  helps energy to circulate freely through your chakras.
- Close your eyes and become aware of the rhythm of your
  breathing. After a few moments, change to breathing as
  for grounding and energy running (see page 20).
- When you feel what should by now be the familiar sense
  of becoming calm and grounded, focus your breathing
  into your heart chakra. Sense your heart chakra like a
  rose that is about to open. Its outer petals are spring
  green, whilst there is a promise of a tender rosy pink
  within and, at the very centre, a touch of gold. It has a
  delicate fragrance. The colours are translucent and
  ethereal, yet the rose itself has substance. With each in-
  breath and out-breath the petals unfold, releasing more
  and more of its fragrance, and the heart centre colours
  surround you. As the centre of the rose reveals itself, you
  see that the base of each petal has a delicate amethyst
  light and tinge, and then a depth of gold in the centre
  that is almost like a gateway inviting you to go deeper
  and further. Your heart centre is pulsating and turning.
- Let yourself gradually be drawn into the golden centre

of your heart chakra. Sense a fine, golden light spreading around you and within you, illuminating your body and your being. Sense an expansion of your awareness. Let this sense of expansion move out towards the plant, crystal, person, animal or tree that you have chosen to work with on this occasion.

- Let the fine golden light surround your contemplative ally (plant, crystal, person, animal or tree). Breathe it out towards them, let it surround them and then breathe it back in to your heart chakra. Feel your rhythm joining with theirs, sense the life force of your ally, be at one with it – have a sense of unity and sharing with it. Let yourself know, in your heart, what it is to be that ally until you are a part of it and it is a part of you. Sustain this part of the meditation for only two or three minutes at first.

- Gradually draw the fine golden light back towards yourself; feel it containing and surrounding you. Become aware again of the rose fragrance and the delicate greens and pinks of the petals of the rose of your heart. Feel a pulsing rhythm within your heart centre that links with the central rhythm of the universe ... with rhythms of earth and sea ... with currents of air ... and with the flicker of flames in a gentle warming fire. Feel your body being healed and vitalised.

- Gradually let the petals of your heart chakra begin to fold in again. Let them just relax, so that the petals retain a resilience, without being too tightly closed or too widely open and vulnerable. See spring green light all around and over the flower of your heart chakra.

- Then, through the rhythm of your breath, return to an awareness of your body, your contact with the ground and your normal everyday surroundings. Visualise a cross of white light in a circle of white light over your heart chakra and draw a cloak of white light with a hood right around you. Feel your feet firmly in contact with the ground and refocus into the outer world thoroughly before resuming your normal tasks.

Exercise
Enhancing Your Subtle Body Layers

This exercise helps to cleanse, strengthen and differentiate your subtle bodies. It is energising, healing and protective, but will also help you as you train your perception to sense, and perhaps eventually see, the six subtle layers of the aura that extend beyond the physical body.

Seven bands of light and colour are breathed around your body from left to right, starting and ending at your feet, then seven more from the back of your body to the front also starting and ending at your feet. The colours are: deep rose pink, amber, golden yellow, spring green, lapis lazuli blue, indigo and deep violet, and should be visualised or imagined as vibrant and translucent – like stained glass, when sunlight passes through it.

Red links to the root chakra and energises the physical body, orange to the sacral and energises the etheric body, yellow to the solar plexus and energises the astral body, green to the heart and energises the feeling body, blue to the throat and energises the lower mental body, indigo to the brow and energises the higher mental body, and violet to the crown and energises the ketheric, causal or soul body.

Eventually you can do this meditation in almost any position or situation, but first practise it standing if possible, or sitting on an upright chair.

- Stand easily and comfortably. Pay attention to the balance of your head on your neck. Place your feet comfortably apart; do not tense your shoulders or lock your knees. Relax any tension in the lower part of your body and rock your pelvis a little until you have a relaxed stance.

- Before beginning to visualise the colours, pay attention to your breathing. Imagine a breath that starts underneath your feet on the in-breath and travels up your left side, close to your body to the crown of your head. Here you start the out-breath, which goes down the right side of your body to the starting position under your feet. Practise these breaths until the rhythm is flowing easily.

- Now, begin the light and colour breaths. Visualising deep rose pink light, breathe a band of this colour up your left side on the in-breath, keeping the colour band close to your physical body. At the crown of your head, change to the out-breath and take the deep rose colour down the right side of your body, letting it join under your feet.

- Do the same with each colour in turn, moving slightly further out from your body as you breathe each new band until you are surrounded with a rainbow of coloured light. Light and colour can interpenetrate with physical matter, so visualise the bands of light lying as evenly under your feet as around the rest of your body. Once you have established the spectrum of light around you in this direction, continue to breathe evenly.

- The next step is to breathe the light and colour bands around you from back to front. Again, you start under your feet, with deep rose pink. Breathe it up the back of your body to the crown of your head on the in-breath and down the front of your body to join under your feet on the out-breath. End with violet, as before.

- When you have breathed all the bands of light and colour from side to side and back to front, continue to breathe evenly and let each band of colour expand and join around you until it forms an egg shape. Imagine a Russian doll effect. You are in the centre, surrounded by seven eggs of light and colour. Feel strengthened, energised, protected and secure.

- Before you take up your normal tasks once more,
  visualise a silver egg of light enclosing the other seven.
  In this way, you take light and energy with you wherever
  you go, but are less vulnerable to any unwanted
  impingement from the outer world.

When you know this exercise well, it is not always necessary
to go through the complete breathing and visualisation –
though it is a good meditative practice in itself. At any time
when you feel vulnerable or in need of an energy boost, you
can merely visualise the seven eggs of light and colour
surrounding you, with the final egg of silver as a container
for the energy and to help you in absorbing all the healing
effect which light and colour can bring. This is also a good
exercise to teach to your patients.

Exercise
Cleansing Your Etheric Field

Since healers are often vulnerable to picking things up from
the environment or even from the psyches of their patient, this
is an important practice for the maintenance of 'healer health'.
It is similar to the aura combing stage of the basic healing
sequence (see page 40), but this version is done through
visualisation and is an exercise for maintaining personal
vitality and clarity. It keeps the etheric web fresh and vital.

You can do the exercise lying down (just before you sleep
or on waking are good times), sitting or standing. One of my
trainee healers said she used it frequently in a bus queue or
on a train platform!

- Become aware of your breathing and your body. Become
  aware of the energy field that stretches beyond your
  body, especially the first or etheric layer, near to
  your physical body, but emanating out from it.

- Imagine that you have a small brush, perhaps similar to a toothbrush, dipped in light, and that you are gently but systematically brushing this first layer of your subtle bodies with light. Imagine it as a fine web that fills with light as you brush. Imagine your body gently enclosed in and protected by this light-filled mesh and that anything that might have been sticky or heavy around you has now been cleansed away.
- Let your heart chakra petals gently close in and then either go to sleep, if you are doing this last thing at night, or begin your day with new energy for whatever is coming next in your life.

Exercise
Sensing the Auric Layers

For this exercise you really need a partner to work with – although you can endeavour to use your hands to sense your own subtle bodies instead or as well. Remember that the intense layers of the auric field are usually all held within about 10–15 centimetres (4–6 inches) of the physical body, so each movement outwards into the six bodies beyond the physical is very slight. It is an attunement to the next level of being.

Though the subtle bodies may be explained, and clairvoyantly seen, as being layer upon layer or layer within layer, to some extent they interpenetrate or intermix with each other. Sensing them is not so much about discovering where one layer ends and another begins as about developing an awareness of the energies that coexist around us.

- Let your partner sit in a chair or lie down, face upwards, on couch or floor. Begin by grounding and running energy (see page 20). Approach your partner from the front, back or either side if they are sitting, and from the side and above if lying. Rub the palms of your hands together to awaken your hand chakras. Ask permission to gently place your hands on your partner's physical body. Make sure they are resting very lightly and then visit several positions on the body, say the shoulders, solar plexus, knees and calves or the feet. Be aware of the warmth and energy of the physical body, which gives out a faint, deep, rosy red colour.

- When you can feel this warmth and perhaps sense or even glimpse the soft redness, move your hands very slightly out from your partner's body so that you are still very close to the body, but not touching it. Try to pick up a prickly sensation with an impression of a clear but delicate orange or amber colour. The prickly, electrically tingling layer is the etheric layer.

- If you have difficulty in sensing the etheric layer generally, hold your hands at either side of your partner's body at the same level as the sacral chakra, and only move elsewhere when you have picked up the electrical, tingling sensation. (Between sensing the subtle body layers you can move back and rub your hands together again, or you can just gradually let your hands move outwards very slightly, as you endeavour to sense each stratum.)

- Move a little way out again, and run your hands over, but off, the body. You are now seeking to experience or sense the astral layer. Remember that this layer is smooth, flowing and cool. Sense the change in texture. The colour can vary from a pale, golden yellow through rose pink to a silvery blue. If, initially, you have difficulty in picking this 'body' up, hold your hands at either side of your partner's body at the solar plexus level, where the vibrations of the astral body tend to be strongest.

- Once more move your hands out very slightly. You are now moving into the feeling body, the third layer out from the physical body. This layer is vital but less fluid than the astral body. It has a softer, warmer texture and glows with delicate light green colours. It can be sensed most strongly on a level with the heart chakra, to which it is strongly connected.

- The fourth layer, moving outwards from the physical body, is the mental body. With connections to the throat chakra, it is sensed most strongly at and around throat chakra level. The mental body is fluid and tingly in texture. It reflects fine blue, silver and turquoise colours.

- The fifth layer or level of the subtle bodies, connected to the brow chakra and therefore most strongly sensed around that area, is the higher mental body. This has a supremely light and subtle texture and glows with pale indigo and amethyst. Its texture is filmy, sheer, pulsating and cool.

- The sixth, or final, level of the subtle bodies is the variously titled soul, ketheric or causal body. It is linked to the crown chakra and may be best sensed around that area of the body. It radiates a pale but intense violet light and its texture is flowing and silky with a soft warm glow.

- When you have finished working with your partner, make an energetic separation (see page 23). It is essential to do this even if you are about to exchange your positions.

When you first try this exercise, you may feel some sensations clearly and others only vaguely or not at all. At first you may feel nothing except the warm radiance from the physical body of your partner. Keep practising! Don't give up! These subtle perceptions have a habit of suddenly becoming clear, easy and natural but can only do so if you persist with the exercises.

Exercises
Drawing Out Negative Energy

This is a useful healing exercise as a variation on those that principally use the chakra points or work more directly with points of pain, discomfort or disease. Called chelation, it helps to blend, balance, integrate and improve the flow of all the fine layers and points in the subtle anatomy of the being. Chelation means 'drawing out'. It draws out toxins and gently sorts out any tangles or knots in the totality of our beings. In practice, it is simple to use, whilst its effects are deep and wide throughout the physical and subtle energy system.

As we have already seen, the chakra points reflect imbalances in the total being and are receptive points for healing of all kinds, but there are other points on the body where any weakness, distortion or confusion in the flow of the subtle energies will show up, and where receptivity to healing and adjustment is strong. Among these are the points used for chelation, which are beneath the feet, in the knees and the knee joint, where the legs join the body, in the hips, at the waist, at the wrists, at the elbows, at the shoulders, at the neck and at the crown of the head.

Chelation is most easily channelled when your patient or a partner with whom you are working is lying down, but may also be given when the patient is sitting on a chair. In chelation, as in other healing sequences, remember to lay your hands very lightly on your patient. Touching too heavily or firmly or leaning on the body will not enhance your patient's healing experience!

Chelation can be practised by one healer, or by two working in partnership. Always prepare for giving a chelation as you would for any other healing, but note the additional preparation and attunement needed if you are working as a pair, with another healer, to channel healing together to one patient.

1. One Healer, Patient Lying Down

- Settle your patient on the floor, couch or bed. If possible you should be able to move right around your patient and be able to stand at the head and at the feet. Make your initial healing preparation and attunement of grounding and running energy and invocation (see pages 20 and 52).
- Begin by standing behind your patient's head and then, having asked for permission to touch the body lightly, gently place both hands on your patient's crown. Hold your hands still until you sense a quietness or balancing happening – or for two or three minutes.
- Now, keeping your right hand in touch with the crown of the head, move your left hand down to the base of your patient's neck at the left-hand side, where it joins the body. Endeavour to sense the energy flow and balance happening between your hand points.
- When a balance or change seems to have happened, or after about two minutes, move your right hand down to join your left at the base of the left-hand side of your patient's neck. Move your feet so that you are not stretching to reach. Basically, during a chelation, you will walk right around your patient, from left to right. A moment or so after having moved your right hand down to join your left at the base of the neck, move your left hand out to your patient's left shoulder and again sense how the flow between your hands helps to balance, move and change the energy.

This sequence of movement, where you heal the flow between two points and then let your hands join on the same point, before separating them again, is essential to a successful chelation.

- After about two minutes, or when you sense a positive healing change, move your right hand to join your left at the shoulder and then, when they have been very briefly at the same point together, move your left hand down to your client's left elbow. Wait again, either for two minutes or until you sense change, and bring your right hand to join your left at the left elbow of your patient. Move your left hand to your patient's left wrist and continue as before.

With the healing pauses, the sequence now continues thus:

- Your right hand joins your left at your patient's left wrist and your left hand moves to your patient's waist.
- After two minutes of healing flow, your right hand joins your left at your patient's left waist and then your left hand moves down to your patient's lower hip.
- After two minutes of healing flow, your right hand joins your left at your patient's left lower hip and then your left hand moves down to your patient's left knee.
- After two minutes of healing flow, your right hand joins your left at your patient's left knee and then your left hand moves down to your patient's left ankle.
- After two minutes of healing flow, your right hand joins your left at your patient's left ankle and your left hand moves down to the sole of your patient's left foot.
- After two minutes of healing flow, your right hand joins your left on the sole of your patient's foot and your left hand moves to the sole of your patient's right foot.
- After two minutes of healing flow, your right hand joins your left on the sole of your patient's right foot and your left hand moves to your patient's right ankle.
- After two minutes of healing flow, your right hand joins your left at your patient's right ankle and your left hand moves to your patient's right knee.
- After two minutes of healing flow, your right hand

moves to join your left at your patient's right knee and
your left hand moves to your patient's lower, right hip.

- After two minutes of healing flow, your right hand
  moves to join your left at your patient's right hip and
  your left hand moves to your patient's right waist.
- After two minutes of healing flow, your right hand
  moves to join your left at your patient's right waist and
  your left hand moves to your patient's right wrist.
- After two minutes of healing flow, your right hand
  moves to join your left at your patient's right wrist and
  your left hand moves to your patient's right elbow.
- After two minutes of healing flow, your right hand joins
  your left at your patient's right elbow and your left hand
  moves to your patient's right shoulder.
- After two minutes of healing flow, your right hand
  moves to join your left at your patient's right shoulder
  and your left hand moves to the base of your patient's
  neck on the right-hand side of the body.
- After two minutes of healing flow, your right hand joins
  your left at your patient's right-hand side base of neck
  and your left hand moves to the crown of your patient's
  head.
- After two minutes of healing flow, your right hand
  moves to join your left at the crown of your patient's
  head. You have now returned to where the sequence
  began and so it is time to round off the healing by
  stepping back and making the energetic separation (see
  page 23).

Your patient will probably feel very relaxed and drowsy
after this treatment, and may like to be covered with a soft
blanket for a while in order to finish absorbing the healing.
When ready, an offer of a glass of water or cup of tea is
usually welcome. Try to end the session quietly, without too
much conversation, before you and your patient move on to
the tasks of normal living.

2. Two Healers, Patient Lying Down

It is supportive and can be stimulating to work with another healer to give a joint healing sequence to one patient. Giving a joint chelation is ideal for this.

The lead healer makes the decisions about when to move on to the next healing position. You and your fellow healer need to be intuitively aware of each other and to make eye contact after about two minutes at each position, so that you can indicate the next move and make it smoothly, together. The lead healer is responsible for initiating the eye contact whilst the fellow healer has to remain alert enough to sense when it is coming.

- When you have made your patient comfortable, decide with your co-healer which one of you is going to be the 'lead' healer for this sequence. Prepare individually, by grounding and running energy, and then stand facing each other and attune your energies by placing the palms of your hands together (right palm to left and vice versa).
- If you are the lead healer, you should stand at your patient's head with your fellow healer at your patient's feet. Having asked permission to lightly touch your patient's body, you, as lead healer, put both hands on your patient's head (as in the first exercise, page 139), whilst your fellow healer puts their right hand on the sole of your patient's right foot and left hand on the sole of your patient's left foot. As you and your fellow healer maintain the position at your patient's head and feet, you will probably become aware of energies flowing and balancing through your patient and of a strong contact with your fellow healer.
- The next move is for you to place your left hand at the base of your patient's neck on the right-hand side, and for your fellow healer to join you at your patient's head

and put their left hand beside your right hand, and right
hand at the right-hand base of your patient's neck.

- After about two minutes of healing flow, make eye
  contact with your fellow healer and, as synchronously as
  possible, move your right hand down to join your left
  hand whilst your fellow healer moves the left hand down
  to join the right. You then move your left hand to your
  patient's left shoulder and your fellow healer moves the
  right hand to your patient's right shoulder.

- After about two minutes, or when you sense a positive,
  healing change, make eye contact with your fellow healer
  and move your right hand to join your left at the
  shoulder. When both sets of hands have been very
  briefly at the same point together, move your left hand
  down to your patient's left elbow, whilst your fellow
  healer mirrors your movement at the right side of your
  patient's body, with their hands complementing yours.
  At your side of the body, right hand follows left and at
  your fellow healer's side, left hand follows right. The
  hands should never cross over each other and the lead
  hand should not leave a chelation point until it has been
  joined, for a moment, by the following hand.

- Wait again, either for two minutes or until you sense
  change, make eye contact with your fellow healer and
  bring your right hand to join your left at the left elbow
  of your patient whilst your fellow healer mirrors your
  movement, with opposite hands, on the other side of
  your patient. Move your left hand to your patient's left
  wrist whilst your fellow healer moves right hand to right
  wrist.

Now continue the sequence:

- After two minutes of healing flow, make eye contact with
  your fellow healer and bring your right hand to join
  your left at your patient's left wrist, then move your left

hand to your patient's left waist. Your fellow healer mirrors these movements, in unison, at the right side of your patient's body.

- After two minutes of healing flow and on eye contact with your fellow healer, your right hand joins your left at your patient's left waist, followed by moving your left hand down to your patient's lower hip whilst your fellow healer mirrors, in unison, on the right-hand side of your patient.

- After two minutes of healing flow and on eye contact with your fellow healer, your right hand joins your left at your patient's left lower hip and then your left hand moves down to your patient's left knee. On the other side of your patient's body, your fellow healer mirrors these movements in unison – left hand joining right at right lower hip and right hand moving to left knee.

- After two minutes of healing flow and on eye contact with your fellow healer, who mirrors your movements on their side of your patient's body, your right hand joins your left at your patient's left knee and then your left hand moves down to your patient's left ankle. (Fellow healer moves left hand to join right at right knee and right hand moves to right ankle.)

- After two minutes of healing flow and on eye contact with your fellow healer, who moves in unison, mirroring your movements, your right hand joins your left at your patient's left ankle and your left hand moves down to the sole of your patient's left foot. (Fellow healer moves left hand to join right at patient's right ankle and right hand to the sole of your patient's right foot.)

- After two minutes of healing flow and on eye contact with your fellow healer, your right hand joins your left on the sole of your patient's foot and your fellow healer's left hand joins right on the sole of your patient's right foot.

- As lead healer, you now lift your left hand from your patient's right foot, but maintain contact with your right hand, allowing your fellow healer to move their right hand to join yours on the sole of your patient's left foot. Once your fellow healer is in the position where their right hand is on the sole of your patient's left foot with their left hand still in contact with the sole of your patient's right foot, you break your contact with your patient's foot and walk quietly up the right-hand side of your patient, back to the position at your patient's head where you began the healing sequence. (You have worked down the left side of your patient's body, but you walk up the right side, back to the head.)

- Put both hands gently on the crown of your patient's head. Make a strong renewed attunement to your fellow healer with their hands on the soles of your patient's feet and then gently, in unison, release the contact and walk away. Make your energetic separation from your patient and also, on this occasion, make an energetic separation from your fellow healer and they from you.

Again, your patient will probably feel very relaxed and maybe drowsy after this treatment. Remember to offer a soft blanket and to allow time for them to finish absorbing the healing. When ready, offer a glass of water or cup of tea. Try to end the session quietly, without too much conversation, before you, your patient and your fellow healer move on.

If circumstances are such that your patient needs to sit on a chair to receive a chelation the movements and sequences are the same and one healer can work alone or two healers together. In order to achieve the position where your hands are under the soles of your patient's feet, it is helpful if the patient has their shoes off and has a foot cushion. (It has been assumed that a prone patient would almost automatically have shoes removed.)

Working in the auric field, with your hands and healing chakras, energy points and subtle bodies, is the main substance of a healer's work, but there are other tools for healing that can be used alongside this basic knowledge to expand and enhance your healing sessions and bring special qualities and benefits to your healing interactions. The next chapter describes and explores some of these.

Chapter 7

Other Tools for Healing

Pauline's story – Considering using tools for healing – Colour –
Crystals – Fragrances – Sounds – Helping others to help
themselves – Absent or distant healing – Exercises

PAULINE'S STORY

Like Robert (see page 118), Pauline was a natural healer
but she had very different difficulties. In some ways her
sensitivities were too open, because she 'tuned in' not only
when healing, but all the time. In everyday life, she found
it difficult to be near other people unless they were family
or very well known to her. She could not watch news
programmes on television or read newspapers easily,
because her extreme openness and psychic empathy would
make her feel ill or depressed when learning of others'
difficulties or suffering. She knew she was a healer, but
hesitated to practise as one because she became too moved
by the thought of her patient's pain or disease. Before she
learned about energetic separation, she would pick up
symptoms if she gave anyone healing, and not just mildly

and fleetingly but quite acutely, perhaps for several days.

When Pauline came to see me, she needed help and healing for herself, but also to resolve an energetic problem that is common amongst healers. I have often observed that unless healers express their ability to heal in some way, they get intensifications and loop-backs of energy in their own subtle systems and find normal life trying, invasive and tiring. Such people need help to control their sensitivities, so that they know how to shut down without shutting off while still being able to open up safely when it is appropriate. Their subtle body layers need strengthening and blending.

In a combination of healing and teaching, I introduced Pauline to the energetic separation exercise (see page 23) and encouraged her to use it for all kinds of purposes: to be less open to others when travelling on public transport or shopping; before watching television and during and after television programmes; when reading the newspapers; as soon as she felt anything impinging on the sensitive feeling layer of her aura, and at any moment when she felt energy was beginning to drain from her. To do this, she had to learn to be aware that the energy drains and increased moments of sensitivity were happening, so that she could help herself before she became completely exhausted.

It is incumbent on all healers to develop a more acute awareness of what is happening to their own energies and to the energetic environment around them. Being sensitive should mean being aware and able to anticipate – and therefore take charge – of things. It should not mean being a victim of circumstance who is continually drained or over-affected by normal life. 'Sensitives' need to be able to manage themselves well enough to participate fully in any and every aspect of life that they might wish to embrace.

Another exercise I taught Pauline to value and practise was the one designed to strengthen your energy field (see page 170) given at the end of this chapter. It is similar to the exercise for enhancing your subtle body layers (see page

132), but has more emphasis on the use of personal, private and public psychic space.

Pauline also needed to learn to give colour to her own chakras so that the 'tone' of their petals was enhanced and they could not flop open so easily and beyond her control. This was especially important for her at her heart chakra.

As she learned to be the one in control of her sensitivities, Pauline found she had more energy and began to enjoy a much fuller life. She also realised that she could practise healing without being drained psychically, emotionally and physically. This was very enabling to her: if 'born' healers practise healing, their own energies benefit and flow more naturally and healthily.

The new adjustments did not happen overnight. As Pauline began to give healing to others again, we looked in the first instance at methods of making the channelling less intensive for her. She found that visualising and channelling colour to patients was less taxing than merely opening as a channel for healing. She had a natural feeling for crystals and fragrances and found that using these in a healing session left her more easily in control of her own sensitivities. (She had also found crystals a great help when learning how to manage her own acute but delicate energy system.)

CONSIDERING USING TOOLS FOR HEALING

There are specialist courses for healers who want to know a great deal about colour, crystals, fragrances and sound, but these are natural healing tools that can be used effectively and safely, by employing a little knowledge and a lot of feeling with extended awareness and intuition.

As a healer, it is a good idea to have a spectrum or palette of skills and alternatives. Not all will be appropriate all the time, and not all will attract you. For some healers, the tools mentioned here may feel like unnecessary appendages. For

others, like Pauline, they can be a help in finding and defining a clearer and more comfortable relationship with
healing energies themselves and with patients' needs and
expectations. It is good to explore what is on offer, but also
good to follow your own evaluation of what is, or is not, for
you.

Using tools for the enhancement and variation of healing
enables healers to use their skills, intuitions and sensitivities
in different ways. For example, when Pauline used colour in
various ways for healing her patients, she found that having
a tool enabled her to become less enmeshed in the healing
process and flow. Some of these tools can also be passed on
to the patient to use for themselves between healing sessions.

COLOUR

Because I believe the chakras to be basic in learning how to
practise healing, colour has already been an intrinsic part of
the healing information in this book. It is extensively
referred to in Chapter 5, where suggestions for visualising
colour as you heal your patients are included.

In addition to learning to visualise and channel colour, I
would encourage healers to acquire simple colour aids that
can be used to enhance the healing environment and
changed according to the needs of individual patients. Using
colour in your general home and life environment, and
suggesting to patients that they use it in this way, is also
important. Pauline found that using colour helped her to
help herself and it can be a fundamental aid to healers' own
health and well-being.

As a non-professional healer, it is unlikely that you will
have a special room set aside for healing, but it is important
to take as much care in preparing the environment as in
preparing yourself for a healing session. That is not to say
that a quick healing session on a kitchen stool or in the living

room before you have cleared up the children's toys is any less effective in terms of transfer of energies, but having respect for your gifts and creating a whole and harmonious healing experience for your patients leads to a very different healer/patient relationship.

When you know that your healing skills are going to be called upon, try to arrange a time when you will be free of other concerns. Prepare a space, even if it is only a corner of a room that is much used for other things, and employ colour to help make that space harmonious.

As healing is mostly a heart-centred function, the colours of the heart chakra are good ones to consider. A pale green or rose cushion for your patient's feet, a green, rose or amethyst-coloured blanket or wrap to put around them during or after the healing sequence, a pink or green candle burning, a few heart-coloured flowers in a suitable vase or a green plant in the area will all help to create an atmosphere and enhance your attunement and your patient's receptivity.

If you are giving a series of healings to a patient with a particular need, you can vary some of these 'props' accordingly. Add deeper rose colours for anyone who needs healing for a structural condition such as rheumatism, arthritis or back pain. Introduce some orange or amber for patients who need extra energy or who are anaemic or rather depressed. Yellow and sunshine gold are helpful to digestive problems, while the heart colours help asthma, breathing difficulties and oversensitivity. Blues are cooling where there is inflammation, and indigos and violets help eyes, head and renewal of hope in life.

Remembering these touches will help your healing to be more specific to each individual and will add to your patients' sense of being seen, heard and cared for. (There are fuller comments on colour symbolism in Chapter 5.)

CRYSTALS

Full crystal healing is a discipline in itself, and there are courses and workshops available for those who want to learn in detail about crystals and their healing qualities. Each type of crystal (and, indeed, each individual crystal) has many different attributes. Studying these can open up whole new dimensions to your healing possibilities. Natural crystals, such as clear quartz, amethyst, rose quartz and aventurine, to name but a few, are reminders to us of the spirit that resides in matter. Used as an aid to spiritual work and healing, crystals enhance and amplify.

At the simplest level, any healer can use crystals as a support to the healing process. An amethyst cluster in the space you use for healing will help to absorb and transform the difficulties that your patients bring in with them. The active healing energies contained in crystals are released when we declare our healing intention and use the crystal to help us focus on that intention or to help in directing the healing flow to a specific bodily area or chakra.

The chakra lists in Chapter 5 and the section here on page 155 give a range of crystals for each chakra but, broadly speaking, crystals are linked to chakras by their colour. Red or dark crystals are for the root chakra and its associated functions, orangey ones for the sacral, yellow for the solar plexus, green for the heart, blue for the throat, indigo for the brow and violet for the crown.

There are hundreds of different types of crystal, and deciding which to acquire can take some thought. It may help to remember that clear quartz 'points' and rose quartz crystals are universal in their use and are particularly useful for healers who are not intending to acquire very specific or specialised knowledge of the use of crystals and gemstones in healing.

Whilst some crystals are rare and fall into the pricey gemstone category, many others are easily found at specialist or 'New Age' shops, and often from market stalls. It is possible to acquire a small selection of simple but lovely crystals without breaking the bank. Once you have decided which varieties of crystal you would like to acquire and found a source or supplier, rely on your intuition to select which of a particular variety is the right one for you and your healing practice.

Spend some time getting to know your crystal. Look at it carefully, handle it and admire it. When you are ready to prepare your crystal for serious work, rinse it under running water several times, allowing it to dry naturally between rinses. Then, if possible, put the crystal on a piece of silk on a flat surface where it will catch as much light as is available, particularly sunlight. Leave it there for at least a day.

When the crystal has been cleansed and charged in this way, design a simple ceremony in which you dedicate it to its healing purpose. Light a candle and hold each stone in your cupped hands, asking that it may aid your healing work.

Without specific training with crystals, you will only be using them as a support to your work. Because some people can be surprisingly anxious about the functions and powers of crystals, always ask your patient how they feel about your introducing crystals to the healing sequence or even into the healing space.

Using crystals can enhance the healing energies you are channelling and help in focusing them to specific areas. With your patient's permission, crystals can be placed or held on or near chakra points, disease points or pain points. Use one crystal at a time and, unless you have had additional training or experience with crystals, do not place or hold them over the body, particularly the chakra points, for more than two consecutive minutes at a time.

Remember that crystals amplify, magnify and focus other healing energies you are giving. As your hands may not be so active in the healing when you are using crystals, it is possible to over-energise (or over-stimulate) a point or area.

Trained crystal healers sometimes use many crystals and leave them lying on the body in special patterns or spreads but, if you are using crystals as a support to your normal healing practice, using one crystal energy at a time is easier to manage and monitor until your knowledge, experience, intuition or special training with crystals are further developed.

If you have a few crystals on a shelf or in a basket, your patients can be encouraged to choose one to hold during a healing session or to put near their feet, and this can be held or placed for the whole session since it is less involved in the direct healing flow.

Clear quartz points are single crystals of clear quartz with one pointed and faceted end and one flat or slightly rounded end. Such crystals can be very clear and beautiful, or have rainbows visible in them when you look into their centres. They can be used for any chakra and any purpose, but are particularly useful for combing the aura towards the end of a healing session. Aura combing is described in the exercise on page 40. It can be done with the tips of your fingers as you move your slightly splayed hands from the crown of your patient's head down to the feet, moving all around your patient as you do so. It can also be done with the pointed end of a clear quartz crystal, which has a particularly cleansing, soothing but energising effect.

After a crystal has been used for healing, it should be washed under running water, dried, and left in a light place until you are ready to use it again.

Crystals help to enhance intuition and creativity. If you decide to use them for healing, you should use your intuition to help you know when and which are appropriate to a particular patient or situation, but here, briefly, are the qualities of the crystals that have been recommended for each chakra in Chapter 5.

Root Chakra

Agate strengthens our sense of purpose and brings a *joie de vivre*. It is helpful to those who fear poverty and deprivation, and it encourages abundance. It helps to strengthen parenting instincts and skills.

Bloodstone is purifying. It helps blood disorders.

Garnet and **alexandrite** are regenerative and help flesh and tissue to heal. They bring comfort to the bereaved and help generally in all times of loss or change.

Onyx gives strength and stamina. It is a good stone for those who feel overburdened by worldly responsibilities.

Rose quartz is a crystal for universal use. It is nurturing and brings a sense of unconditional love.

Ruby vitalises, nourishes and warms. It is the stone to use for healing when there has been a difficult birth, or bonding to the mother has been delayed for some reason.

Smoky quartz promotes calmness, centredness and groundedness. It helps to calm fear, panic or shock.

Tiger's eye enhances creativity, protects in times of danger, helps when challenges have to be met and aids fertility.

Sacral Chakra

Amber energises, balances and heals. It lifts depression, and aids dreams and creativity. It is useful for healing the female reproductive organs and for helping to regulate the menstrual cycle.

Aventurine helps to release blocked creativity and to activate the imagination.

Citrine heals wounded emotions and promotes emotional maturity. It helps where sexual problems and wounding have to be addressed.

Jasper is a stone of power and empowerment. It helps the oversensitive and those who have obsessional thought patterns.

Moonstone protects all who travel on water. It aids us in gaining contact with our feelings and in being able to see ourselves more as others see us.

Topaz aids fertility and promotes inner peace.

Solar Plexus Chakra

Apatite aids concentration and intellectual thought, and the development of logical communication.

Calcite comes in many different colours. The orange, honey and yellow varieties are most appropriate to the solar plexus and aid psychic development. They help to connect the higher will to the lower will.

Citrine is also mentioned at the sacral centre. Bright yellow shades of citrine help in cultivating clarity, warmth and a sense of self. It also helps the digestive system.

Iron pyrites aids all levels of assimilation and encourages the discovery of true potential.

Kunzite aids self-discipline, self-respect and inner balance.

Malachite aids psychic and spiritual abilities and the remembrance of dreams. It is also healing for physical eyesight problems.

Rose quartz helps to keep the solar plexus flexible.

Topaz strengthens vision and purpose but also aids cheerfulness and humour.

Heart Chakra

Amber purifies the heart and aids the development of balance and love.

Azurite aids compassion and is helpful in healing allergies and asthma.

Chrysoberyl comes in many forms and colours, including the emerald. These stones are comparatively rare and rather expensive to acquire, but they attract kindness and generosity. They are revitalising and therefore are sometimes called the 'stone of perpetual youth'.

Emerald helps to bring about that balance of heart and mind that leads to wisdom. It encourages the development of loyalty, trust and love.

Green calcite heals the subtle bodies and particularly the feeling body. It heals wounds of the heart and helps to bring strength during periods of change or transition.

Jade (green or white) helps to regulate the heartbeat and to increase vitality, longevity and life force. It also aids the development of serenity, wisdom, harmony and perspective.

Tourmaline has a wide range of colours including black. The rose or watermelon varieties are most suited to the heart chakra, where they aid tolerance, flexibility, compassion and transformation. They promote harmony and non-judgementalism. They help the heart when it has to bear trauma, loss or bereavement.

Throat Chakra

Aquamarine eases fears and phobias. It aids positive communication with large audiences and is therefore an excellent stone for writers, journalists and people who work in the media.

Lapis lazuli aids expression of all kinds. It is helpful to the healing of deafness.

Sapphire is said to enable communication with other planets. It strengthens the throat chakra and nurtures the gift of prophecy or channelling and mediumship.

Sodalite, which is often mistaken for lapis lazuli but lacks the gold spots that distinguish lapis, is excellent for healing all inflammatory throat conditions and the thyroid gland.

Turquoise aids the search for true purpose and enhances clarity in communication.

Brow Chakra

Amethyst enhances spiritual awareness and encourages vision. It is a protective stone and transforms negativity.

Azurite is an aid to rituals and blessing ceremonies, as it enhances sacredness. It promotes visionary dreams and helps to harmonise the relationship between spirit and matter.

Blue fluorite is protective. It is a psychic shield, valuable in developing transcendent states of consciousness.

Calcite strengthens the higher mental body. It links the world of spirit with the world of intellect and ideas.

Pearl is for purification and also aids serenity and devotion.

Purple apatite stimulates all levels of perception and aids meditation.

Sapphire strengthens spiritual awareness and communication. It facilitates connection with guides and angels.

White fluorite strengthens the incarnate spirit and helps to prevent depression and disillusionment.

Crown Chakra

Celestite aids meditation and heals and fortifies the petals of the crown chakra. It awakens our desire to celebrate the spiritual aspects of life.

Diamonds are for perfection and clarity. They draw us towards our highest spiritual potential and encourage the higher will to illumine the personality.

Snowy quartz heals resentment and loneliness. It strengthens the soul body but also encourages a 'feet on the ground' approach to life.

White jade awakens the inner divine spark and strengthens communication with the higher self.

White tourmaline encourages integrity and facilitates the deeper understanding of spiritual surrender and obedience. It promotes inner honesty and insight.

Alter Major Chakra

Carnelian encourages contact with nature spirits (see Glossary, page 194). It aids memory of previous lifetimes and the dreaming of positive dreams.

Fossils help us to connect with the wisdom that is stored in the collective unconscious (see Glossary, page 193). They promote a natural and relaxed approach to life, incarnation and evolution.

Peacock stone (sometimes called bornite or chalcopyrites) aids the recall of skills which have been known and practised in another lifetime. This particularly applies to remembering or reviving ancient healing skills.

Snowflake obsidian is linked to the cycles of life, death and rebirth and gives stamina for all times of change.

Tiger's eye enables greater contact with the earth and its rhythms and seasons. It will help herbs to grow in your herb garden, if shallowly 'planted' alongside them.

FRAGRANCES

You would rarely use fragrances directly to enhance your healing sequence at a first session with a patient, but in a general sense it can be helpful to have lavender fragrance in your healing space. This is calming, cleansing and aids energetic separation (see page 23). As with all fragrances, you should aim for it to be subtly rather than powerfully present. A drop of lavender essential oil in a small bowl of water, a delicately fragranced lavender candle, or a fine spray of lavender water on the palms of your hands before you begin healing are all ways to bring fragrance into the space.

Cautions About Using Fragrances

True aromatherapy is a specialised form of healing and you should therefore use fragrance quite tentatively. Without specialist knowledge, refrain from using essential oils with women who are pregnant. If you are intending to use fragrance in a session, you will need to ask any woman patient of child-bearing age whether there is any possibility that she could be pregnant. (Lavender oil as part of the general ambience is excepted here.) You will also need to check with your patient that they are not particularly susceptible or allergic to any aromas. It is a good idea to try out particular fragrances for yourself before using them with clients, so that you can judge how intense they may become.

Using Essential Oils

These considerations aside, once you get to know the nature of a patient's specific needs, the judicious use of a little fragrance, in the form of an essential oil, can be very beneficial to support the healing sequence. Essential oils are pure plant and flower extracts and are very concentrated. One of the best ways to use them in the healing environment is to burn just a drop or so in an oil burner or diffuser.

It is important to use the type of diffuser that allows you to float the oil on water. The oil itself should not be burned or heated directly. Overheating an oil can change its character and may alter the fragrance and its benefits. When using oils on your own hands, mix a drop or so of essential oil with a carrier oil such as sweet almond or jojoba.

Although joss or incense sticks are available in most essential oil aromas, I do not recommend using these in the healing room. They often give off smoke and the fragrance can become quite heavy and pervasive, especially in a small space. They can be good for cleansing a healing space before or after a healing, but avoid burning them during an actual healing sequence.

Essential oils also have links to chakras. When considering whether the gentle use of fragrance might or might not be beneficial for a patient, remember that there are stimulating and quietening oils for each chakra. As you learn to 'read' chakras you will often pick up a sense of under- or overactivity.

An overactive chakra feels excited and tingly or tense when attention is focused into it. Such a chakra may also be open and vulnerable. It needs calming and quietening, and one of the calming oils or a mixture of those recommended can be used to help this process. An underactive chakra will feel 'cold' and closed. It will be difficult to sense a response from it. It needs stimulating and encouraging and one of the stimulating oils for that chakra, or a blend of those given, can be used to achieve this.

As you familiarise yourself with the essential oils, I would encourage you to rely on your intuition about what to use and when to use it, although you should always take the cautions mentioned above into consideration. Use the fragrances in the environment around your patients or on your own hands as you heal gently on the body or in the auric field. Leave it to specifically trained people to put the oil-borne essences directly on the skin or to massage with them.

SOUNDS

The relationship of sound to healing is being constantly researched. Sound healing has also become a discipline in its own right and you can attend workshops and courses to learn about it. However, you do not have to be trained in sound healing in order to consider using it to support your own healing practice if you use it in a gentle way and always consult your patient before doing so.

I have often discussed with healers on healing courses the issue of whether or not to play music during healing sessions. My own view is that taste in music can be very personal, that it is not always easy to reproduce it with good quality, and that it is difficult to know at what volume it becomes intrusive. If it is either too soft or too loud it can become an irritant rather than an asset. I would not choose to play music during a healing session or to have it played when I am the one being healed. This is a personal view-point and, as with so many things, healers must eventually choose for themselves what works best for them and their patients, and be prepared to learn from experience.

I often play music to prepare myself before giving a healing session, or to help in preparing the healing space. Music of the Baroque period is conducive to healing vibrations and the slow movements from Mozart concertos have a particularly healing vibration. Apart from the classics, there is a wide variety of tapes and discs that have been prepared by intuitive, healing and musical people. Explore the field, and sense what is right for you, and use it accordingly for your own meditation, for cleansing or preparing your healing space, and perhaps as you are making your healing attunement or rounding off for a patient.

Using Musical Instruments

A healing sequence that you might add to your repertoire is given in the exercise on page 172. For this you need to collect a selection of musical instruments, which could include a drum, a rattle, a rainstick, a triangle, a bell and a singing bowl. The sounds these instruments make are cleansing and harmonising to the subtle bodies and the chakras. The drum restores natural rhythms, the rattle helps to clear unwanted thoughts, the rainstick clears toxins and is particularly useful for people undergoing chemotherapy or radiotherapy, the triangle and bell are also cleansing and balancing, and the singing bowl helps people to attune to their true selves and their chakras so that these balance individually and in relationship to each other.

Practise with any instruments you acquire until you are familiar with them and can make sounds that are reasonably controlled. With a drum you should be able to sustain a gentle, rhythmic sound that should not be drummed more slowly than the normal heartbeat. Fast, loud drumming is a shamanic (see Glossary, page 194) healing practice and is best avoided unless you have specifically studied that area.

Rattles

Rattles are shamanic instruments but with practice you can shake one gently and consistently around your patient's aura or over chakras to help the patient be free from worries or obsessions.

Rainsticks

These simply need turning from end to end in order for their cleansing sound to flow. Be careful when selecting your rainstick that the sound made as the materials inside it flow from end to end is reasonably sustained and does not start too suddenly or end too abruptly.

Triangles

Although you might feel that triangles belong mainly to the infant school percussion band, they have a very pure sound that disperses and rebalances energy in the subtle bodies and around the chakras. Practise until you can strike yours accurately enough to get its clearest sound as often as possible. You can then strike it over organs or chakras to clear blockages, or in the auric field for cleansing and clearing.

Healing bells

A healing bell should be light and bright in tone and is usually quite small and light in itself. Choose one that is pure and pleasant in its tone and it will function, in healing, in a similar way to the triangle.

Singing bowls

Singing bowls are not cheap to acquire. Some are old and some are modern. When choosing, be guided by your own response to the sound. Generally, the larger the bowl the deeper the note. True singing bowls are made of brass and come from Tibet. You need a simple, lathe-turned wooden striker or baton to go with them. This can be used in two ways.

Whilst holding the bowl on the palm of your hand, but without any fingers touching its sides, gently strike the bowl two or three times with the baton. Because of the construction of the bowl, the sound will sing on and on and on ... Having started the resonance with the striker you can then run it gently around the top of the bowl, with the striker held vertically and in touch with the bowl. It takes exploration and practice to be able to sustain this movement at the right speed and pressure. If you go too fast or have an uneven pressure, the striker will squeak against the bowl and interfere with the true resonant note.

When you become really expert at the movement of the striker around the top of the bowl, you do not need to strike the bowl to set the resonant note going, but can simply move the striker around the bowl until it starts to sing and keeps on singing. Singing bowls can be sounded over chakras, organs and in the auric field for purposes of harmonising, cleansing and balancing.

When to Use Musical Instruments

The sound chelation (draining of negative energy) is the main way to use sound to support your healing practice. But you can start and/or end a healing session with the chime of a bell or triangle, or the sound of a singing bowl. You can do the same thing at any time during a healing sequence, to aid clearance (but warn your patient beforehand that this might happen!).

You can use any instrument you may have available in your healing space, for a few moments, as your intuition guides you. Practise with a friend or a partner to help you first, and note your reactions to the instruments. Sound is a serious, supportive, healing intervention, but have fun with it too!

HELPING OTHERS TO HELP THEMSELVES

One of the best ways of supporting your healing practice is to be aware of the tools that you can pass on to your patients, so that they can further their own healing between any sessions they have with you.

It is important that patients do not assume that, having found a healer, they can or must hand everything over to you. This is particularly relevant when people have a long-term illness or condition. Attitudes in allopathic medicine are gradually changing but it has tended to give us the message that we are wrong to want to be involved in the decisions that are made about treating our illnesses. However, engagement with our own healing journey is important.

Knowing that there are tools that can help us towards a positive outcome of disease helps us to remain in a place of choice and autonomy. Your patients need you, and will put a lot of faith and hope in your abilities. From very early on in the healing process it is good to hand back some of the responsibility for their healing by asking patients to work on themselves and their healing between sessions and by re-assuring them that they can do so effectively.

It is said that good teachers not only impart information but teach us how to learn. It might also be said that good healers not only impart healing but teach us how to heal ourselves.

Exercises That Patients Can Use

A number of the exercises given in this book are not only suitable for you as a developing healer, but are also applicable for your patients to practise too, in the interests of self-healing. One of the most healing things for Pauline (see page 147) was to learn about energetic separation. It is not uncommon for many of us today to feel that the rush and crush of ordinary life impinges upon us in a way that adds to our stress, especially if we are ill or worried.

Energetic separation (see page 23) helps us to maintain our own space. It can also be used to help us to separate from difficult experiences – not in the sense of denying them, but in the sense of keeping a separate strength and wholeness with which to deal with them. I have known chemotherapy patients who have used energetic separation successfully to be able to say: 'I am not the chemotherapy. The chemotherapy is not *me*. It is a treatment that will enable me to get well again.'

Energetic separation can also be used to help in dis-identifying with an illness (not denying it). In the English language we have too many statements that say: 'I *am* ill'; 'I *am* lame'; 'I *am* deaf'; 'I *am* angry.' Such statements subtly imply that we are no more than our illness or our emotions. Consciously substituting *'have'* for *'am'* and using the energetic separation exercise can work remarkably to put us in a greater position of choice when it comes to managing the condition we have. We do not 'become' a condition, and we do not have to lose contact with our true selves. We can always maintain choice and jurisdiction.

The exercise relating to analysing illness and the sick self (see page 88), is one that patients can be encouraged to explore in order to understand more about the underlying dynamics of their illness and to realise that making life and attitudinal changes are important to total healing and health.

The exercise for enhancing your subtle body layers (see page 132) can also be taught to patients. If they practise it at least once between sessions, their auras will become much more receptive to healing energy and some of the balancing of colours and chakras will be in hand, so that your healing in sessions can become more specific, direct and immediate rather than the supportive and general level taking a major proportion of the healing time and energy. (This will automatically happen if your patients have done some self-work between sessions and therefore come to you with a more resilient aura.)

Two of the exercises later in this chapter are helpful to patients. The exercise on strengthening your energy field (see page 170) is as useful for patients as it is for healers, while the meditation exercise (see page 173) is specifically designed as a self-healing meditation.

Frequency of Healing Sessions

Some of your patients may only come for one healing session, while others may come for a series. Obviously, you will vary the frequency of healing sessions according to the patient and your own intuition, but they should not usually be more than once a week unless someone is very ill or has a short-term acute condition when even daily healing can be appropriate. The spaces between healing sessions are important to healing absorption. Too much dependence on you as a healer should be discouraged in favour of helping your patients to take more responsibility for self-healing. When the healer is redundant, the patient, hopefully, is well.

Preparing Tapes for Self Healing

In the early stages, patients may press for greater frequency once they feel that you are able to help them. Having a tape with a self-healing meditation, given in your voice, will help them to have an interim connection with you, whilst also working towards their own healing. Reading the meditation exercise (see page 173) on to tape can be a start here, but as you gain confidence you can design your own healing meditations and personal tapes to give to patients in order to encourage this important self-involvement.

Quite short tapes can be made to help patients to relax. Taped instructions about feeding colours into appropriate chakras can be useful to encourage self-work between sessions. You might tape yourself talking a particular patient through a meditation at the beginning of a healing session and then offer the tape to be taken home and used between visits. Or you could make a tape of the induction for the colour meditation exercise (see page 107) and the exercise at the end of this chapter (the induction is the first two paragraphs of the exercises). You might then suggest that your patient breathes some spring green and pink colour into the petals of the heart chakra before moving on to another chakra or body part that you feel would benefit from colour or attention.

Suggesting Crystals, Fragrances and Sounds

You can introduce your patients to crystals and suggest they get one or two appropriate ones to have in their environment to remind them of a colour useful to their general healing process. A crystal at the bedside can help patients to remember to ask for healing before sleeping. You can also suggest that crystals be held over chakras or pain and disease points for a few moments each day – but emphasise that a maximum of five minutes is enough when holding a crystal over a chakra point, although they can be left on pain areas for longer. In addition, you can show patients how to comb their own auric field with a clear quartz point.

If your patients respond well to fragrances that you have introduced into the healing room or used on your hands when healing, you can suggest that they get a suitable essential oil and a carrier oil. Advise them to mix a few drops of essential oil into the carrier oil and then use this mixture as an addition to bath oils, as a skin fragrance or for gentle massage of painful parts.

Patients with whom you have used sound might be keen to have one of the simple instruments mentioned above in their own homes. Listening to the true, clear sounds made by these is healing in itself and can clear an atmosphere or a mood.

Using Absent Healing

Finally, you can offer to put your patients on your absent healing (see page 169) list, particularly if you incorporate a practice of spending ten or twenty minutes daily or two or three times a week using this healing focus. Having a set time for them to 'tune in' is helpful. I simply light healing candles at 9 pm each day and spend a quiet time remembering all those who have asked for healing flow and thought.

ABSENT OR DISTANT HEALING

Returning to my belief that all natural healers need to be involved in healing in order to be healthy in themselves, absent or distant healing is helpful if you do not have time, space or inclination to heal patients directly. Pauline, for example, found it a help to do distant healing for and with friends before she felt strong enough to give hands-on healing.

Absent or distant healing works very well. Some of your patients may not be able to come to you for healing as often as might be desirable. Others may be family members or friends living at a distance. Arrange to have a quiet time in which you 'think' or intuitively direct healing energy towards them or 'hold them in the light'. A group of you may gather together at a regular time to send out absent healing to individuals, to world leaders or causes, to animal, mineral and plant kingdoms, and to the substance of earth itself.

Light a candle and maybe have a favourite crystal beside you. Do the grounding and running energy practice. Make a healing invocation, including in this the angels of light and love and healing.

Say aloud, three times, the name of the person for whom you are requesting healing, without saying why they require the healing or dwelling on any symptoms you know them to have. Imagine that person surrounded with golden light. After about three to five minutes of focus and concentration, see your distant healing patient fit, well and following their favourite pursuits.

You can extend and amplify this healing ceremony by lighting a small candle or night light for each person or concern to which healing is being sent. At the end, as you extinguish the light or lights, think of the light being sent out rather than putting a candle out. See streams of light flowing towards those to whom healing has been given and see them as whole and healthy.

It is best to get people's permission before sending them absent healing, but since this is general rather than specific healing, a holding in light rather than a defined intervention, you can also use it for those who are too ill to make a personal request or where others have requested healing for a loved one.

Exercise
Strengthening Your Energy Field

This exercise helps to develop and strengthen your energetic temple of being, which defines personal, private and public space.

- Making sure that you will be undisturbed, sit or lie in a comfortable but symmetrically balanced position. Wrap yourself in a blanket for comfort and warmth if you wish, remembering that in meditation, your body may lose heat. Unless you are sitting cross-legged or in a lotus position, do not cross your legs at the ankles or knees. Do not fold or cross your arms. Have the palms of your hands open and curved, and facing upwards. You can balance your hands, palm open and up, on your knees if you are sitting and on the floor or couch beside you if you are lying.
- Be aware of the rhythm of your breathing – don't force your breath or try to calm it. Simply allow it to find its own natural rhythm. Gradually bring that rhythm into

your heart centre or chakra and sense how each in-
breath and out-breath feeds, relaxes and opens your
heart chakra.

- Enter your inner space and imagine yourself sitting at a
  central, beautiful, peaceful place within a larger temple.
  This is your inner sanctuary and you can spend some
  time creating it and making it as you want your inner
  sanctuary to be. Beyond the inner sanctuary there are
  many courtyards, each of which is associated with a
  different colour. Your inner sanctuary will be white,
  gold, silver or violet in essence, but you can also add any
  other favourite colours.
- Your sanctuary is sacrosanct, and none may enter here,
  unless you invite them specifically. There will probably
  be very few to whom you would extend that invitation.
  Your guardian angel (see Glossary, page 193) helps you
  to guard this sanctuary and to maintain its inviolability.
- Move out of your sanctuary to explore the courtyards.
  Those near to your sanctuary are open only to people or
  influences you know and trust, and those further away
  are open to the potential for new acquaintances and new
  experiences, but by filtering these through the
  courtyards and meeting them always outside your actual
  sanctuary, you protect yourself from invasion, give
  yourself time for assessment of others and also make sure
  that you are being seen as you want to be seen. There
  may be an association with elements in the courtyards or
  with music, poetry, art and fragrance.
- Enjoy creating and exploring your inner sanctuary.
  Return to it whenever you feel vulnerable. Know that
  there is always a central space that is yours and yours
  alone, and that you can keep other concerns and
  meeting places in the courtyards most appropriate to
  them.
- Return to the breath in your heart chakra and to your
  awareness of your body. Put a cloak of light with a hood

right around you and return, without rushing, to your
everyday world and tasks.

Exercise
Drawing Out Negative Energy Using Sound

For this healing sequence you should choose an instrument
from those mentioned above with which you are familiar
and which you have practised using beforehand.

To draw out negative energy (see page 138), you move
around the patient paying attention to energy points at the
head and the feet and at the main joints of the body. For
sound chelation the principle is the same, but you make
sounds with your chosen instrument over the energy points
and also around the body as you move between the energy
points.

- Have your patient either lying down or sitting up. Do
  your grounding and running energy preparation (see
  page 20).
- Standing at the patient's feet, rattle gently at the crown
  of your patient's head (if you are using a rattle, for
  example), then pause, before rattling down the left side
  of the head to the base of the neck.
- Rattle at the base of the neck, pause and then rattle out
  to the left shoulder, rattle over the left shoulder, pause
  and then rattle down to the left elbow.
- Rattle over the left elbow, pause and rattle down to the
  left wrist. Rattle over the left wrist, pause and rattle in to
  the left waist.
- Rattle over the waist, pause and rattle down to the point
  where the left leg joins the body. Rattle over this point,
  pause and rattle down to the left knee.
- Rattle over the left knee, pause and rattle down to the
  left ankle. Rattle over the left ankle, pause and rattle

down to the sole of the left foot. Rattle over the sole of the left foot, pause and rattle over to the sole of the right foot.

- Rattle over the sole of the right foot, pause and rattle to the right ankle. Rattle over the right ankle, pause and rattle up to the left knee. Rattle over the left knee, pause and rattle up to the point where the right leg joins the body.

- Rattle over this point, pause and rattle up to the right waist. Rattle over the right waist, pause and rattle out to the right wrist. Rattle over the right wrist, pause and rattle up to the right elbow.

- Rattle over the right elbow, pause and rattle up to the right shoulder. Rattle over the right shoulder, pause and rattle up to the right-side base of the neck.

- Rattle over the right-side base of the neck, pause and rattle up to the crown of the head. Rattle over the crown of the head, pause and rattle down the centre of the body to the feet. Rattle over the feet, pause and rattle up the centre of the body back to the crown of the head.

- Rattle once more over the crown of the head, put your instrument down and make your energetic separation (see page 23).

Exercise
Using Meditation to Heal Yourself

This is a good exercise to promote your own health as a healer (see Chapter 8). It is also a good one to teach to your patients and can be used as an absent healing meditation, where you hold others in the rainbow light.

- Make sure that you are not going to be disturbed. If possible, light a candle and dedicate it to your healing. Sit or lie in a comfortable, symmetrical position and become aware of the rhythm of your breathing. Within the breath rhythm become aware of your heart chakra. Feel the petals of your heart chakra opening, allowing the heart energy to flow.

- Travel on the heart breath into your inner space and imagine yourself walking along a wooded pathway. The ground is soft under your feet and the fragrance of leaf mould is around you. Sun is dappling through the trees and you can hear the sound of the water.

- Soon, through the trees, you see a busily babbling stream and you walk towards it. You decide to follow the stream, walking in the direction from which it is flowing. As you come out of the wood, the ground is drier and quite stony. You are going gently uphill. Now there are some bigger rocks around you and you become aware of a waterfall somewhere near. You come upon the waterfall rather suddenly. It is splashing down from some higher rocks into a natural pool, from which the stream runs. The sun is shining and a misty spray rises from the water. In the sunlight, the spray is full of rainbows.

- You find a smooth rock, which has been warmed by the sun. As you sit on it, you realise that you are being bathed in rainbow healing light. Sit for a while and let the light flow over and into you. Feel it going to any place where there is pain or unease. Feel the vitality that it brings. When you feel ready to do so, you will get up and make your way back alongside the stream to the woody path where this journey began.

- Before you leave the place of the waterfall, wash your hands and perhaps drink from the clear water in the pool. In the depths of the pool there may be a gift for you – a symbol to help you on your healing path.

- After your return to the wooded path, become aware of the rhythm of your breathing and of your heart centre. Enter the outer world once more. Blow out your candle.

Let the flower of your heart centre close in a little and visualise a cross of light in a circle of light as a blessing over it.

This chapter has introduced ideas and practices that may be more appropriate for the more experienced healer running a healing practice for patients other than family and friends, but it is always a good idea to aim for a professional standard, even in informal surroundings and with people you know well. If you want to expand beyond working with family and friends, there are practical and professional considerations you will have to address. The next chapter on the health of the healer looks at some of these, and at the important transition from 'non-professional healer' to fully practising professional healer.

Chapter 8

Becoming a Professional Healer

Keeping it simple – Practical considerations – Who heals the healer? – Will I need some allied skills? – Referral to other agencies – Keeping well in body, mind, emotions and spirit – Using meditation

KEEPING IT SIMPLE

Having started with a simple approach to healing, it may seem that more structure and more knowledge is bringing with it more complexity. Most healers that I have known and worked with become fascinated by the whole complex and absorbing subject of healing. They keep learning more and more, both from their own experience and from teachers of healing. Yet, having tried many healing sequences or different types of intervention, they almost invariably return to something quite simple and direct.

As one healer said to me: 'There is a place for doing things with crystals and sounds and different energy points, but mostly I just want to be clear and simple and channel the energy that I know I can bring through me.' I agree entirely, but also maintain that the simplicity that comes at the end of the journey is different from the simplicity that makes the journey necessary. The simplicity of a certain naivety can be beautiful and direct, but the simplicity that is also informed is like a clear well-spring arising, full of nutrients, from the depths.

The journey to greater knowledge may also awaken in you the desire to be more than a healer for family and friends, and to look for further training, with the aim of having a professional practice where people pay for your services. If this is the journey you want to take, there has perhaps not been a better time to take it. There are many outlets and opportunities, but also professional and practical considerations.

PRACTICAL CONSIDERATIONS

Once you move into the professional field, having a healing corner at home, or knowing you can clear a suitable space when required, is not enough. You need somewhere more permanent, or you may want to hire a room for a few sessions in a natural health centre.

When you are considering wider and more professional practice, the question of 'answerability' in the wider sense arises. This is more than mere loyalty and wanting to do the best for your patients. You will need insurance. In order to get this you must belong to a healing organisation or have gained a recognised healing qualification. There are some useful addresses on pages 196–7 to help you find out where to train and what sort of training is available.

You cannot really be paid until you have some kind of professional standing but, in my experience, healers have great difficulty with the subject of payment and so I should like to set out some considerations here. Even with family and friends, it is a good idea to have some kind of barter or exchange. This is a boundary issue. Difficulties always arise if one person is the constant giver and the other the receiver. If there is a meaningful exchange, the patient feels freer to ask for a repeat treatment and the healer is less likely to feel a draw from or incursion into their time and space.

Of course, healing is an energy, not a medicine. It is freely available within the structure of the universe, not manufactured and packaged. Of itself, it cannot be priced. Yet if you are to heal as more than a hobby, to a point where perhaps you need to leave your job, reduce your working hours or spend considerable time away from your family commitments, then the time you give to the work has to be valued, as is any professional's time. Doing courses can be expensive and it is reasonable to expect that these could be funded from your healing practice once it gets more serious.

Money, in our times, is a convenient form of exchange. If you are receiving a service then you expect to pay for it in some way. So, once you feel you are professional, look at what your needs are and set an appropriate fee for healing by the hour or half-hour. If you do not absolutely have to earn from the healing, it still benefits those who receive to be able to give or return something. Some healers put out a donation bowl or a charity box.

WHO HEALS THE HEALER?

One of the benefits of courses and training is that healers meet each other, form friendships and sometimes heal each other or give each other support. If you are a 'lone' healer, try to find a group that you can sometimes meet or work with, where skill and support are shared. (Some of the addresses given on pages 196–7 will be helpful here.)

Counsellors and therapists are always expected by their professional organisations to be in 'supervision'. This does not mean that they are perpetual students or probationers but that, because of the complexity of the issues and relationship that can arise between counsellor/therapist and client, there needs to be someone who can advise, support and help in keeping a perspective, with confidentiality honoured and protected.

I should like to see more healers using this sort of consultancy too. Dealing with people who are ill, perhaps with serious diseases, perhaps facing death, can be a heavy weight to carry. Supervision gives healers a point of reference and support and helps them to 'debrief' and maintain a necessary warm detachment from some of the problems patients bring.

WILL I NEED SOME ALLIED SKILLS?

Many patients want to tell their experiences in full, and having them heard can be an important part of the healing process. Working with the symbolism of disease (Chapter 4) can be very helpful, as can designing meditative exercises and affirmations as part of a self-help programme. Ideally then, healers should consider developing some counselling or listening skills.

You do not have to be a fully fledged counsellor, but knowing the most helpful ways of listening to and drawing a patient out can be a bonus. Acquiring some facility in this area will also help you in knowing when it might be a good idea to suggest to a patient that they have some sessions with a therapist or counsellor. Courses in these skills are usually readily available at local colleges of education.

Some healers train in one of the complementary skills, such as reflexology, aromatherapy or massage, and let their healing skills flow through the discipline of the treatment. For some patients such therapies are more easily acceptable and less challenging than the thought of 'energy' or 'spiritual' healing.

REFERRAL TO OTHER AGENCIES

Referral to other agencies is an issue that healers should keep in mind. Once you are working with people who are not well known to you, it is wise to upgrade your knowledge of basic first aid and of symptoms that need medical attention (see Appendix, page 189). Practicality and healing must go side by side, if healers are to be respected. If there has been an accident, it is good to be channelling healing whilst basic first aid is done, but not good to be doing nothing but channelling healing when urgent mouth-to-mouth resuscitation is required.

Healers often have patients who are seeking energy or spiritual healing as a last resort, having tried everything else and there being no further medical treatment possible. More and more, though, people come to healers before this sad stage is reached. They seek the support of healing whilst receiving other, more conventional treatments. I have often worked with cancer patients who appreciate healing and counselling as aids to minimising the unpleasant side effects of radiotherapy or chemotherapy.

Patients should always be supported in the choices they are making about their management of their illnesses. They should be encouraged to see their doctors, not discouraged. Healing is not an alternative therapy, but a complementary one. Many doctors are open to it and welcome the information that their patients are also seeing a healer for support. Some medical practices have healers available at the surgery for those patients who want this.

Always try to persuade your patients to tell their doctors that they are receiving healing. As you become more highly trained and professional, you should consider always asking your patients' permission for you to inform other carers that their patients are working with you.

KEEPING WELL IN BODY, MIND, EMOTIONS AND SPIRIT

Most healers, especially when they are healing on a regular basis, feel well and are full of energy in themselves. Having the opportunity to channel healing is as vital to a healer as having the opportunity to run is for a dedicated runner (as we have seen in Pauline's story, see page 147). Pauline's oversensitivity was partly due to the nature of her giftedness but, once she understood the principle of energetic separation, she realised that she could more easily manage her own energies so long as she could practise her healing.

This situation of a potential imbalance of energies in a healer who has no opportunity to heal, who has resistance to being a healer or who has not recognised the gift as such, is not a question of healing sapping the healer's own vitality. One of the questions most frequently asked by patients after a healing is: 'Does it drain you?' The answer to this should be an emphatic 'No'. The energy that is healing is a channelled energy, with the healer naturally having the special sensitivities that allow that to happen or having developed them through training.

As a healer you are constrained to heal because it is what you are for, or about. You don't have to be a hands-on healer to satisfy that urge to heal. Many healers at work in our society would not call themselves healers in the sense in which the word healer has been used in this book.

From Parliament to the law courts, in schools and hospitals, in therapy rooms, in the business of everyday life, on buses and trains, in offices, shops and bars, in homes and families everywhere, healers abound. Their leadership, justice, caring, ability to listen, sense of humour, quiet presence or creation of harmony has that extra ingredient of healing – you feel better for having seen, travelled with or visited them. Such are the 'hidden' healers in society who consciously or unconsciously have found a satisfying way to express what they have to express. They are rarely subject to energetic discomfort.

Realising that you are a healer uncomfortable with your own sensitivities, but with no opportunity to develop your gift, may mean that you have to seek other ways of channelling healing than the hands-on variety. There are ways of managing and sublimating until you can make the life changes that may be necessary for honouring your gift. Whatever you are involved in and cannot change, you can do it in a more healing way or from a more healing perspective.

I was a reluctant school teacher. When I eventually realised that I wanted to heal, not teach, I felt even more dissatisfied. Being a single parent with a young child meant that there were practical reasons why I could not easily change my life at that point. It was only when I realised that I could still see myself as a healer, although I needed to go on teaching for a while longer, that I adjusted more smoothly to my teaching career than I ever had before.

Others around me in my professional life probably noticed little, if any, change – I continued to teach as before. But for me, things changed a lot. I sought opportunities to make the teaching environment a healing one and to bring implicit healing into my relationships with staff, children and parents. I created a different ambience in the classroom with colour and the arts. I tried to let the healer flow through the teacher, rather than seeing the teacher as repressing the healer.

A friend of mine also longed to work with healing and was particularly interested in the healing use of colour. Again, there were practical considerations preventing her from leaving her rather boring office job. Although 'stuck' in an office, once she identified herself as a healer she found ways to bring in colour, harmony, plants and flowers. Suddenly her co-workers began to remark that they enjoyed coming to the office, because its atmosphere was so cared for.

In keeping well as a healer, the first consideration, then, is to respect and name yourself 'healer'. This opens the gateway to finding expression for your true self, and to gaining satisfaction from so doing.

A second consideration is to own the sensitivity you have in order that you learn better how to manage it. Many sensitives say, 'I don't want to become, or to seem, precious.' In fact the more you take care of and make provision for your sensitivities, the more 'normally' you can function in everyday life. If you do nothing to manage your susceptibilities, then you will become easily exhausted, bothered by crowds and overstressed by daily living. The energy exchange can be important to the healing flow and needs serious consideration. If you heal too often in your 'spare time', you will become unable to sustain what you have set out to do. One thing healers have to learn to avoid, in every sense, is getting stressed or 'burning the candle at both ends'.

The management is very simple:

1. **Remember to ground and run energy at least once a day**, whether you are about to be involved in giving hands on healing, or not (see page 20).
2. **Remember and understand the principles of energetic separation** and use them frequently (see page 23).
3. **Allow time for yourself.** As others become aware that you are a healer, they may expect you to 'turn it on' at a moment's notice. Except in real need, try never to do this. If you have gone out for an evening, to a friend's for supper, or if the friends have come to you, it is unwise to suddenly mix a healing session with the social one unless it has been previously arranged.

    Such happenings make boundaries unclear and a healer's sensitive constitution needs clear boundaries. 'Yes, I will willingly give you some healing tomorrow at 10 am' is a more appropriate response to the spur of the moment request than to put your prospective patient on a stool in the midst of a crowded kitchen and give healing immediately. If you are socialising, socialise. If you are healing, set proper boundaries and keep it as a separate activity.

4. **Never imagine that putting strong shields of light around you and staying vulnerable inside them is the way forward**. You need strong and supple subtle bodies, and strong chakras that close and open their petals with ease, neither staying too tightly closed, nor being overblown and too full in their opening.

    This means that you need to practise not only the central column breathing (see page 20) but also to feed your individual chakras with their 'home' colours (red for the root, orange for the sacral, yellow for the solar plexus, green for the heart, blue for the throat, indigo for the brow, violet for the crown and brown for the alter major). Practise the subtle body enhancing exercise (see page 132) and cleanse your etheric field (see page 134).

5. **Keep a balance in your life.** Have ordinary mundane fun, enjoy creature comforts and celebrate your normality as well as your special gifts.

6. **Resolve to learn more about meditation** and bring some meditational practices into your life (see page 173 and Further Reading, page 195).

7. **Take care of your own health and well-being** in every possible way. It is a myth that healers have to be complete models of good health, perfectly free from difficulties of their own and free from disease or tendency to disease. Generally you need to feel vital and alert enough to be able to channel healing energy towards someone else. If you have an infectious cold, cough or other transitory illness, it is best not to be in the close contact with patients that giving healing requires. When you are ill, get healing from your fellow healers and where necessary use medical treatment. The grounding and energetic separation exercises (see pages 20 and 23) will help to keep you in good health, as will the self-healing meditation (see page 173).

USING MEDITATION

Most healers have a natural aptitude for meditation and inner journeying, and experience slightly altered states of consciousness when giving healing. Even if you do not consider yourself to be a 'natural', the art of inner exploration can be developed with time and patience.

Once commonly practised only in Eastern religions, meditation has become increasingly recognised in the Western world for its health-giving, stress-relieving and creativity-enhancing benefits, as well as for spiritual attunement and to assist in the search for mystical experience. Yet confusion still arises as to what exactly meditation is. Essentially it is an altered state of consciousness in which a range of subtle physiological and mental changes help to bring about a feeling of serenity. Some industrial companies provide opportunities for personnel to learn meditation so that the burdens of decision-making may be eased and new, creative ideas come from a place of inner peace.

The practices by which the meditative state is achieved are often confused with the state itself. Alternate nostril breathing, breath counting, breath watching, visualising a rose, or chanting a mantra while watching a candle flame are all means to an end.

In the meditative or ruminative state we become receptive, our perceptions are subject to delicate change and the less conscious reaches of our beings are more easily accessible. Thoughts, feelings, memories, images and symbols, which may have been partially or wholly hidden, gently come to the surface to be recognised, owned and examined, whilst the meditative state enables a centredness and non-attachment that helps us to know truths about ourselves whilst maintaining an inner equilibrium.

The healer who acquires the discipline to practise meditation regularly acquires the ability to centre and focus. When healing, a knowledge of meditation enables outer concerns to be left aside more quickly so that the perceptions of healing can be experienced more clearly and attended to more effectively.

If you have some regular practices as a healer, such as grounding and/or meditation, you will support your own healer identity and strengthen your subtle energy field, but discipline is an interesting subject in itself. I believe it should be gently acquired rather than rigorously enforced. Too much pressure renders the psyche resistant or defensive.

Establish a rhythm for your own spiritual practice that is comfortable and manageable alongside the other commitments in your life. Try not to make demands on yourself which are phrased along the lines of: 'Every morning at 7 o'clock I will always meditate and practise my grounding exercises.' The day or life phase will inevitably come when you fail to meet your appointment with yourself and a 'failure seed' may be sown.

If you take the attitude that, whenever possible, you will meditate each day at a time that is regular but fits in easily with the rest of your life, then each time you keep an appointment with yourself and your support for your healer identity, you will be sowing the seeds of success. Your practice will then grow regular for positive reasons and will bring you joy rather than coming from a rigorously imposed or artificial self-requirement. (Books on meditation are recommended in Further Reading, see page 195.)

Guided journeys and inner explorations require, but also enable, a slightly altered state of consciousness in which the focus of our attention is inwardly directed. Progressively they help us to become more familiar with what is inside – or what is often termed the 'inner landscape'.

You might like to make a tape-recording of some of the longer meditative exercises or explorations given in this book. Leave appropriate pauses, so that you can play the tape to yourself as you meditate or journey without having to remember long sequences. If you tape the meditation you can also time it, and so know exactly how long you need to set aside. Then you need not become anxious about losing track of time.

At the beginning of each meditation, you are advised to make sure you will be undisturbed. It is common for the body to lose heat in meditation, so wrap yourself in a blanket for warmth and comfort or have one to hand in case you need it.

A standard cross-legged or lotus position is excellent for meditation. Your body forms a natural pyramid shape and the subtle energies flow well whilst being contained. If you are not comfortable in either of these positions and prefer to sit more normally on a cushion, on the floor, on a straight chair or armchair, or to lie down on the floor or a bed, it is important not to cross your legs at the knees or ankles. Have your body symmetrically arranged in a way that is relaxed and comfortable.

The lotus position used in meditation.

Keeping the legs uncrossed when sitting or lying other than in a true cross-legged or lotus position allows energy to flow freely without blockage or crossed polarities. For the same reasons, you should not cross or fold your arms. Have the palms of your hands open and your fingers together but curved and facing upwards. Balance your hands, palm open and up, on your knees if you are sitting and on the floor beside you if you are lying. This hand position helps you to be energetically balanced but receptive.

In the induction to each inner journey in this book you are guided to open up your heart centre or chakra. The heart energy is a particularly safe and wise energy on which to travel. Activating it ensures that your experiences will be vivid but gentle. Visualising folding in the petals of your heart chakra, as a protection, at the end of a meditative visualisation (see Meditations Using Colour, page 107) helps to make the transition between inner and outer worlds. The folding is soft, leaving the petals flexible and the chakra open enough to normal life without being either tightly shut down or wide open and vulnerable.

Meditation and inner visual practice is useful to healers. From your own practice of meditation and visualisation you will gradually gain enough confidence to give your patients short inner exercises to do in order to aid self-healing and to sustain them between healing sessions (see Chapter 7).

May you and your healing flourish and this book have proved useful in helping you to be the healer you would like to be.

Appendix

Symptoms Needing Medical Referral

Cardiovascular
Chest pain on exercise.
Blackouts.
Ankle swelling and shortness of breath.

Respiratory
Persistent chest pain.
Shortness of breath.
Coughing up blood.
Weight loss.
Prolonged wheezing attacks.

Gastrointestinal
Vomiting blood.
Passing blood from the rectum.
Passing a sticky black motion from the rectum.
Persistent diarrhoea, especially with blood and slime.
Abdominal pain, especially with vomiting and nausea.
Change of bowel habit.
Weight loss.
Jaundice.

Genito-urinary

Passing blood in the urine.
Burning pain on passing urine.
Severe loin pain.

Men

  Discharge from the penis.
  Difficult flow or inability to pass urine.

Women

  Abdominal pain on intercourse.
  Vaginal bleeding after intercourse, between periods and after the menopause.
  Breast lump.
  Urinary incontinence, especially on coughing or laughing.
  Acute abdominal pain with missed menstrual period.

Hormonal

Weight loss, palpitations, tremor, protruding eyes.
Weight gain, lethargy, coarsening hair and skin.
Thirst, weight loss or gain.
Infertility.

Neurological

Double vision.
Headache with nausea and vomiting.
Weakness of limb function.
Blackouts.

Rheumatology

Severe pain over the temples with pains in the neck and shoulders (in rheumatology patients, these symptoms may lead to blindness).

Skin

Pigmented moles increasing in size.
Pigmented moles with irregular outline.

Pigmented moles with variable pigment density.
Pigmented moles with itch or bleeding.
Lesions on the face, especially in eye, nose and cheek area.

Eyes
Painful red eyes.
Sudden loss of vision.

Ears, nose and throat
Fleshy swelling within the nostril.
Prolonged pain in any of these areas.
Hearing loss.

Orthopaedic
Acute bone pain at a specific site.
Hip pain or limp in children.
Curvature of the spine.

Glossary

Akasha/ether This is usually considered to be a fifth element. There is a progression from the tangible earth, water, fire and air, to the intangible akasha, or ether. It is like a collective energy body for humanity, holding the imprint of everything each individual, group, family or race has ever known, done or is in the process of knowing and doing. It is also thought to have a relationship to the origins of sound and colour. Akasha is approximately the same as that which Jung described as the 'collective unconscious'. Ether is not related to the chemical element but to the term 'the ethers', which is sometimes used to describe other energetic planes and levels.

Angels Angels are direct reflections of Divine Consciousness. They are intermediaries and guardians helping the divine plan to manifest on earth.

The elemental/devic/angelic hierarchy or lifestream may be seen as moving from the divine consciousness towards earth, while the human stream of consciousness, which includes discarnate guides, may be seen to be moving towards reunification with the Divine. The elemental/devic/angelic hierarchy is therefore separate from humanity. Discarnates are not angels, and angels will not take on human form or consciousness. Our guardian angels are different from our discarnate guides and mentors. (*See also* Guardian angels.)

Altered state (of consciousness) Electrical cycles in the brain can be measured. When we are dealing with everyday functioning and the material world, there is a 'normal' range of cycles, known as the 'beta' rhythms. When we sleep, we are mainly in 'theta' rhythm. When, in waking consciousness, we are being particularly creative, 'alpha' rhythms may be present. Through meditation or hypnosis we may enter 'altered' states, in which beta rhythms fade, whilst alpha, delta and theta rhythms become more constant. In such states our physical bodies relax, and we are more open to healing and we may have an expanded awareness in which the barriers of time and space are lessened.

Drugs may induce altered states, but the cumulative side effects and other factors which often accompany drug-taking make them undesirable and usually counter-productive in any serious spiritual exploration.

Archetypes By dictionary definition these are 'primordial images inherited by all'. Each human society is affected by forces such as peace, war, beauty, justice, wisdom, healing, death, birth, love, power. (These are sometimes called 'The Archetypes of Higher Qualities'.) The essence of these defies definition and we need images, myths, symbols and personifications to help us in understanding their depth and breadth. Tarot cards, which have ancient origins, have twenty-two personified or symbolised archetypes in the major arcana. These cover all aspects of human experience. (*See also* Tarot.)

Bach Flower Remedies Edward Bach, a doctor in the last century, discovered that sun-potentised essences of flowers could be produced and would work subtly to heal individuals and their emotional and physical illnesses or conditions. He produced thirty-eight flower remedies; still popular today, they are available from most health-food shops together with leaflets explaining their properties and uses.

Collective unconscious This term comes from the work of C.G. Jung, the psychologist. It refers to the collective bank of human experience. Everything presently happening in our world affects us, although we are only consciously aware of our own 'little patch'. Moreover, everything that has ever been experienced or accomplished by humanity, historically, is also stored. Myths and symbols can help us to tap into the creative collective unconscious. Nightmares, anxieties and irrational fears may be activated by collective, rather than personal factors.

Guardian angels We each have a guardian angel who watches over us from before birth and accompanies our passage through death. Our guardian angel evolves from the elemental hierarchy to accompany us on our journey when our soul decides to take on another incarnation. When we die our guardian angel moves on to some other angelic task. (*See also* Angels.)

Higher Self Our higher self is, in essence, the part of our consciousness or soul which does not incarnate. The higher self has an overview of all our lifetimes and decides our task and purpose in each incarnation.

Nature spirits These are tiny beings generally associated with plants, trees, the natural environment and the elements. They are sometimes called 'elementals'. They appear to those who have clairvoyant vision as points of light or colour, or in traditional fairy form as nereids, sylphs, gnomes, elves, undines, goblins and flower fairies.

Since the four elements interact in our physical bodies and largely determine our health patterns, elementals are within and around us. The giving and receiving of energetic healing activates and encourages them to help us to health and harmony.

Shamanic/shamanism This refers to a tradition and healing form that originated in Iceland and parts of Russia, and also came to be practised by the North and South Native Americans. Shamans undergo rigorous training which enables them to become seers and healers and in full consciousness to cross the boundaries between the planes. Neoshamanism is a reawakening of the shamanic tradition.

Tarot The Tarot is an ancient form of cards that can be 'read' for the purposes of divination. The seventy-two cards form a major and a minor arcana. The major arcana consists of twenty-two archetypes covering all aspects of human experience. The minor arcana has four suits, differently named in different versions of the cards, but mostly representative of mind, body, emotions and spirit – or earth, air, fire and water. The twenty-two archetypes of the major arcana are: the Fool, the Magician, the High Priestess, the Empress, the Emperor, the Hierophant, the Lovers, the Chariot, Strength, the Hermit, the Wheel of Fortune, Justice, the Hanged Man, Death, Temperance, the Devil, the Tower, the Star, the Moon, the Sun, Judgement and the World.

Transpersonal therapy and counselling This addresses the spiritual and behavioural needs and aspirations of human beings. It concentrates on the importance of finding a meaning in life and of being creative and fulfilled in living, relating and making choices.

Further Reading

Titles by Ruth White
Working with your Chakras, Piatkus, 1993.
A Message of Love, Piatkus, 1994.
Working With Guides and Angels, Piatkus, 1996.
Chakras – A New Approach to Healing Your Life, Piatkus, 1998.
Your Spiritual Journey, Piatkus, 1998.

Other Titles
Maxwell Cade and Nina Coxhead, *The Awakened Mind: Biofeedback and the Development of Higher States of Consciousness*, Element, 1987.
Sonia Choquette, *Balancing Your Chakras*, Piatkus, 2000.
C.J. Cooper, *An Illustrated Dictionary of Traditional Symbols*, Thames and Hudson, 1979.
Eric Harrison, *Teach Yourself to Meditate*, Piatkus, 1993.
Soozi Holbeche, *The Power of Gems and Crystals*, Piatkus, 1990.
Richard Lawrence, *The Meditation Plan*, Piatkus, 1999.
Lawrence LeShan, *How to Meditate: A Guide to Self Disovery*, Bantam, 1984.
Katharina Raphaell, *Crystal Enlightenment*, Aurora Press, 1986.
Katharina Raphaell, *Crystal Healing*, Aurora Press, 1987.
Shirlie Roden, *Sound Healing*, Piatkus, 1999.
Eddie and Debbie Shapiro, *Meditation for Inner Peace*, Piatkus, 1997.

Useful Addresses

Ruth White can be contacted on 01273 584060 for information, or please visit her website at www.ruthwhite-gildas.co.uk

British Complementary Medicine Association (BCMA)
PO Box 2074, Seaford, East Sussex BN25 1HR.
Tel: 0845 3455977
(Lists of courses and options open to complementary healers.)

The College of Psychic Studies
16 Queensberry Place, London SW7 2EB.
Tel: 020 7589 3292
(Extensive library, lecture programme, courses.)

Confederation of Healing Organisations (HO)
The Red and White House, 113 High Street, Berkhamstead,
Hertfordshire HP4 2DJ.
Tel: 01442 244296
(Information about healing groups and training, and legislation
about healing and healers.)

National Federation of Spiritual Healers (NFSH)
Old Manor Farm Studios, Church Street, Sunbury-on-Thames,
Middlesex TW16 6RG.

Tel: 01932 783164
(Healing groups; training for healers; monthly newsletter; probationer scheme for healers.)

White Eagle Lodge
Newlands, Brewells Lane, Liss, Hampshire GU33 7HY.
Tel: 01730 893300
(Training for healers, library and literature.)

College of Healing
Runnings Park, Croft Bank, West Malvern, Worcestershire WR14 4DU.
Tel: 01684 566450
(Healer training and other workshops.)

Index